LONDON'S ROYAL PARKS

MALCOLM TAIT
&
EDWARD PARKER

THE
ROYAL
PARKS
FOUNDATION

A Think Book

First published in Great Britain in 2006 by
Think Publishing
The Pall Mall Deposit
124-128 Barlby Road, London W10 6BL
www.think-books.com

Published in association with
The Royal Parks Foundation
The Old Police House, Hyde Park, London W2 2UH
www.royalparksfoundation.org
Registered Charity Number 1097545

Words by Malcolm Tait
Photographs © Edward Parker, Alamy, Giles Barnard, Clare Bowen,
City of Westminster Archive Centre, Corbis, FLPA, Mary Evans Picture Library,
Nigel Reeve, Howard Sooley, Quest Design.
Image on pp 4-5 © UK Perspectives
Design by Lou Millward and Jes Stanfield

ISBN-13 978-1-84525-014-0
ISBN-10 1-84525-014-1

Printed & bound in Singapore by KHL Printing Co.

Cover image: Robin Rawstorne

This book is dedicated to the millions
of people, past and present, who have
planned, played in, managed and enjoyed
The Royal Parks of London, and to the
further millions who will continue to shape
their future in the centuries ahead.

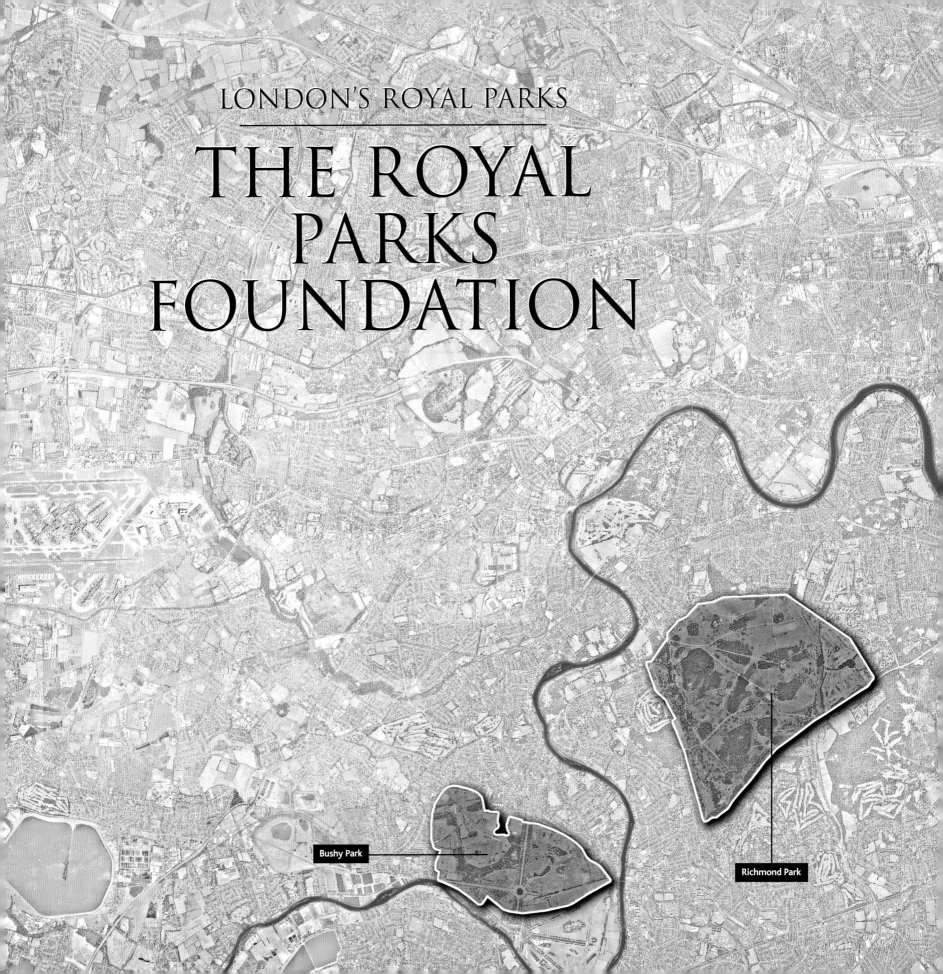

LONDON'S ROYAL PARKS

THE ROYAL PARKS FOUNDATION

Bushy Park

Richmond Park

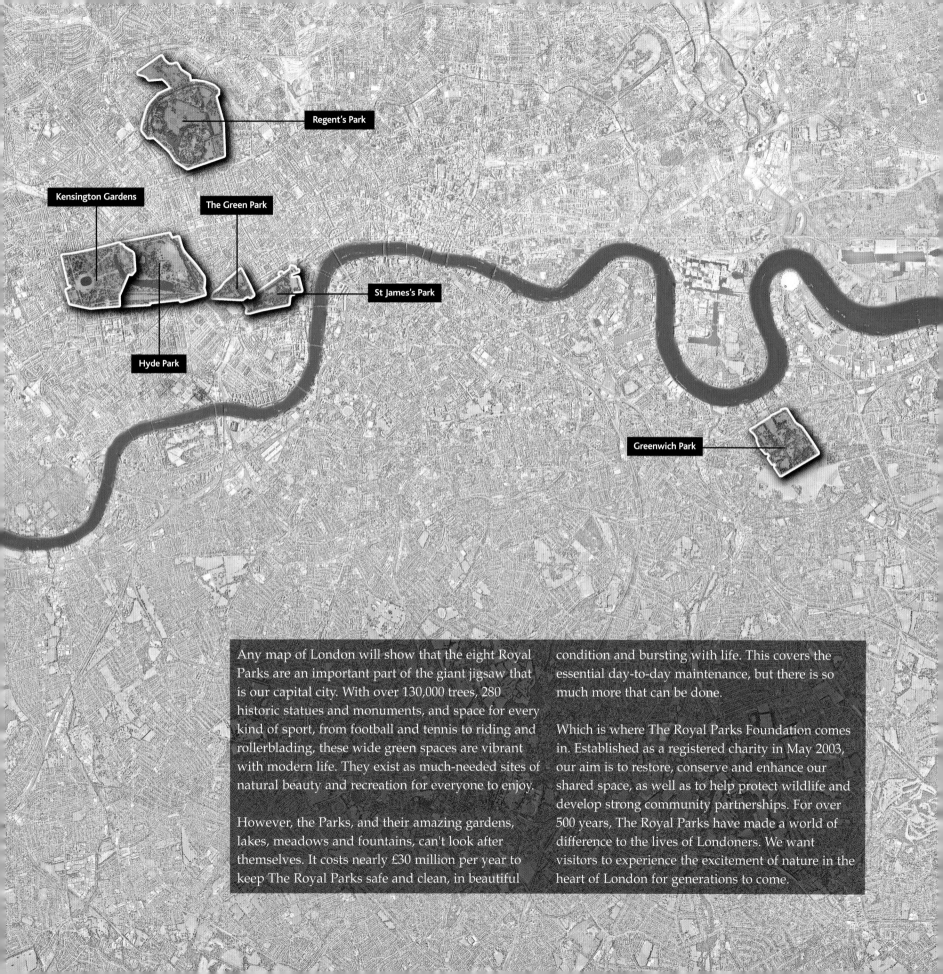

Regent's Park

Kensington Gardens

The Green Park

Hyde Park

St James's Park

Greenwich Park

Any map of London will show that the eight Royal Parks are an important part of the giant jigsaw that is our capital city. With over 130,000 trees, 280 historic statues and monuments, and space for every kind of sport, from football and tennis to riding and rollerblading, these wide green spaces are vibrant with modern life. They exist as much-needed sites of natural beauty and recreation for everyone to enjoy.

However, the Parks, and their amazing gardens, lakes, meadows and fountains, can't look after themselves. It costs nearly £30 million per year to keep The Royal Parks safe and clean, in beautiful condition and bursting with life. This covers the essential day-to-day maintenance, but there is so much more that can be done.

Which is where The Royal Parks Foundation comes in. Established as a registered charity in May 2003, our aim is to restore, conserve and enhance our shared space, as well as to help protect wildlife and develop strong community partnerships. For over 500 years, The Royal Parks have made a world of difference to the lives of Londoners. We want visitors to experience the excitement of nature in the heart of London for generations to come.

LONDON'S ROYAL PARKS

CONTENTS

ROYAL PARKS

WELCOME TO THE ROYAL PARKS

The Royal Parks of London are a fascinating dichotomy.

On the one hand, they are quite literally living reflections of Britain's rich, vibrant and often stormy history of social change. Across their combined 5,000+ acres can be found reminders of the times when Church and Crown eyeballed each other's power with envy and nervousness; of the later years when powerful regal dynasties made decisions based on national security, empirical strength and sometimes just pure whimsy; of the exciting times of enlightenment, education and exploration of unfamiliar sciences and worlds; of the more recent periods of reform as new social classes began to develop a say in the way in which their country was run; and of current democratic political structures and international trade and communications systems which have turned the world into the global village that it is today. Effects and reflections of hundreds of years of fluctuating fortunes and power struggles abound across the parks via their buildings, designs, aspects and functions.

Yet the parks have become reminders of all these lustily lived centuries despite themselves. While the world rages on around them, the function of the parks of London has been to offer a constant refuge from that very strife and toil. Kings and

Bushy Park

Hyde Park

The Green Park

Richmond Park

queens, politicians and scientists, working men and women, locals and tourists, all in their time have sought in the parks brief respite from the struggles of the everyday, and many have left something behind – a building, a new tree, a footprint – to mark their time there.

Thus it is that the hideaways of history have, ironically, become mirrors of that very history from which they offered an escape.

For there's no doubt that escape is what the parks provide. They have always been oases of beauty, stimulation and contemplation within the hurly-burly not just of London life, but of working and personal lives, too. Once, kings hunted in them to help them forget briefly about threats from ambitious dukes or impoverished war chests, and thereby take time to relax and refresh themselves for the challenge. Today, accountants, shop assistants and students lunch in them for the same reason – except that vexing dukes are now replaced by difficult colleagues or exams, and empty war chests by departmental budgets.

Ask 100 people who use any of the parks frequently why that park is important to them, and you'll get 100 different answers. Some go for the buildings or perhaps the wildlife, others for the views or an event; others still for exercise or sport. But each of those answers is likely to contain one similar sentiment: 'going to the park gives me a chance to get away, to think, to be myself'.

Millions upon millions of people have 'been themselves' in the Royal Parks of London throughout the centuries, and by doing so, have helped turn the parks into what they are today, and what they will become tomorrow. This book is a celebration of those people just as much as of the parks themselves.

Malcolm Tait, January 2006

Kensington Gardens

Greenwich Park

Regent's Park

St James's Park

THE ROYAL PARKS

1,000 YEARS OF HISTORY

1086
'Hyde' is first mentioned in the Domesday book as the name of a manor on the Thames.

1433
The Duke of Gloucester fences in a stretch of land above the Thames, making Greenwich Park the first to become enclosed land.

1529
Acquisition of Hampton Court Palace and its surrounding parks by Henry VIII from Cardinal Wolsey. These parks were later combined and are now known as Bushy Park.

1205

1485

1086

1205
King John grants an area of land to female lepers, where a hospital is built called Sisters of Saint James in the Fields. This land will later be known as St James's Park.

1433

1485
Henry VII defeats Richard III at the battle of Bosworth. One of his first deeds upon becoming king is to rename west London's Manor of Sheen as Richmond after the town in Yorkshire.

1529

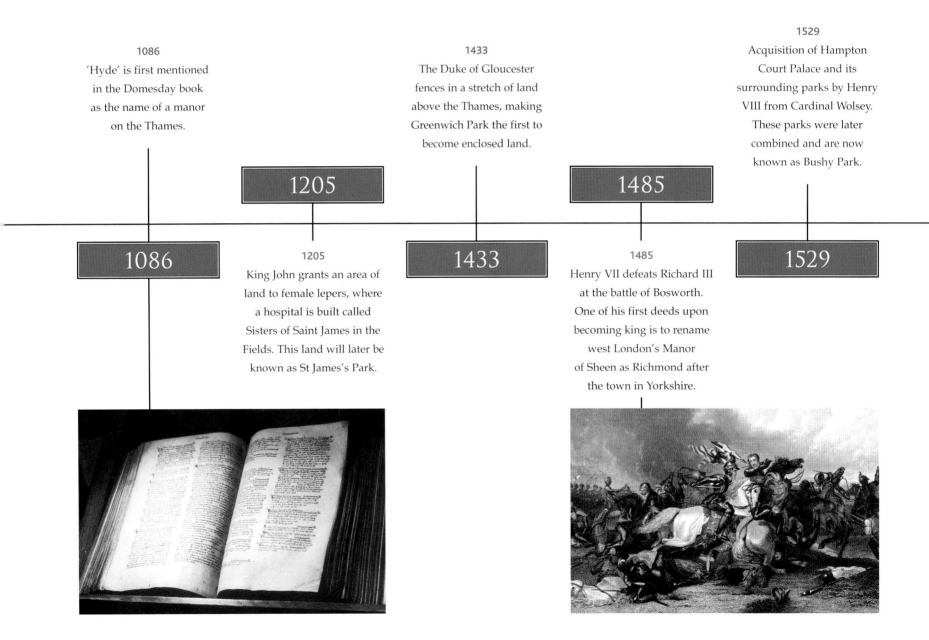

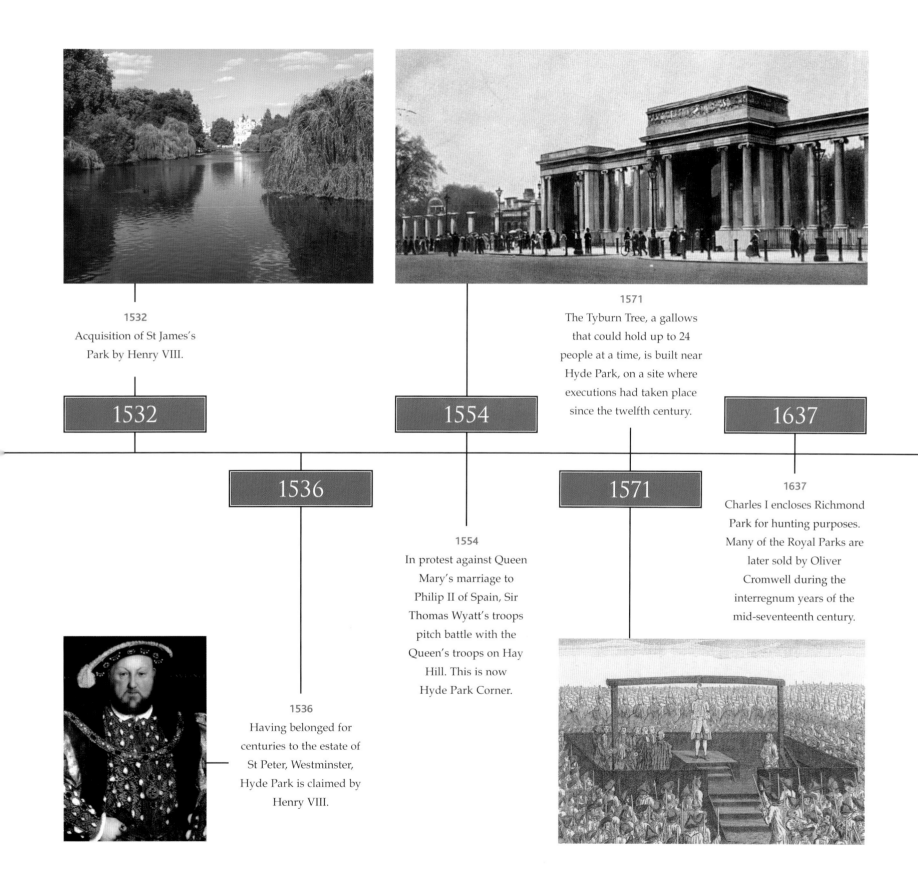

1532
Acquisition of St James's Park by Henry VIII.

1571
The Tyburn Tree, a gallows that could hold up to 24 people at a time, is built near Hyde Park, on a site where executions had taken place since the twelfth century.

1532

1554

1637

1536

1571

1637
Charles I encloses Richmond Park for hunting purposes. Many of the Royal Parks are later sold by Oliver Cromwell during the interregnum years of the mid-seventeenth century.

1554
In protest against Queen Mary's marriage to Philip II of Spain, Sir Thomas Wyatt's troops pitch battle with the Queen's troops on Hay Hill. This is now Hyde Park Corner.

1536
Having belonged for centuries to the estate of St Peter, Westminster, Hyde Park is claimed by Henry VIII.

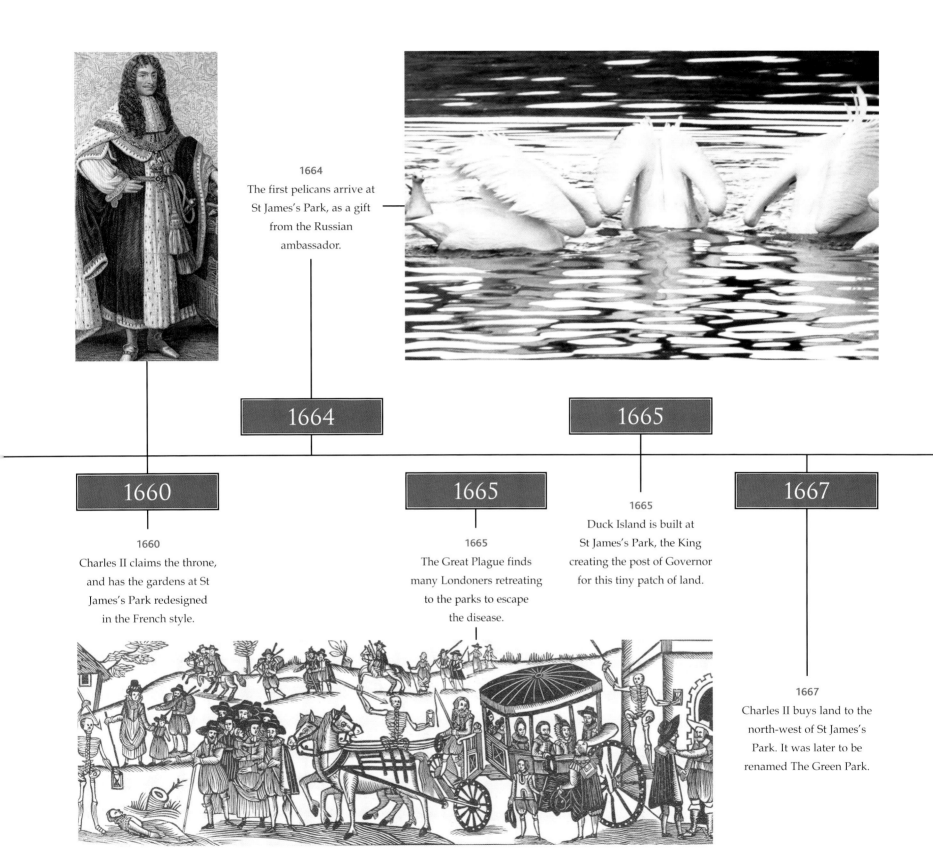

1664
The first pelicans arrive at
St James's Park, as a gift
from the Russian
ambassador.

1664

1665

1660

1665

1667

1660
Charles II claims the throne,
and has the gardens at St
James's Park redesigned
in the French style.

1665
The Great Plague finds
many Londoners retreating
to the parks to escape
the disease.

1665
Duck Island is built at
St James's Park, the King
creating the post of Governor
for this tiny patch of land.

1667
Charles II buys land to the
north-west of St James's
Park. It was later to be
renamed The Green Park.

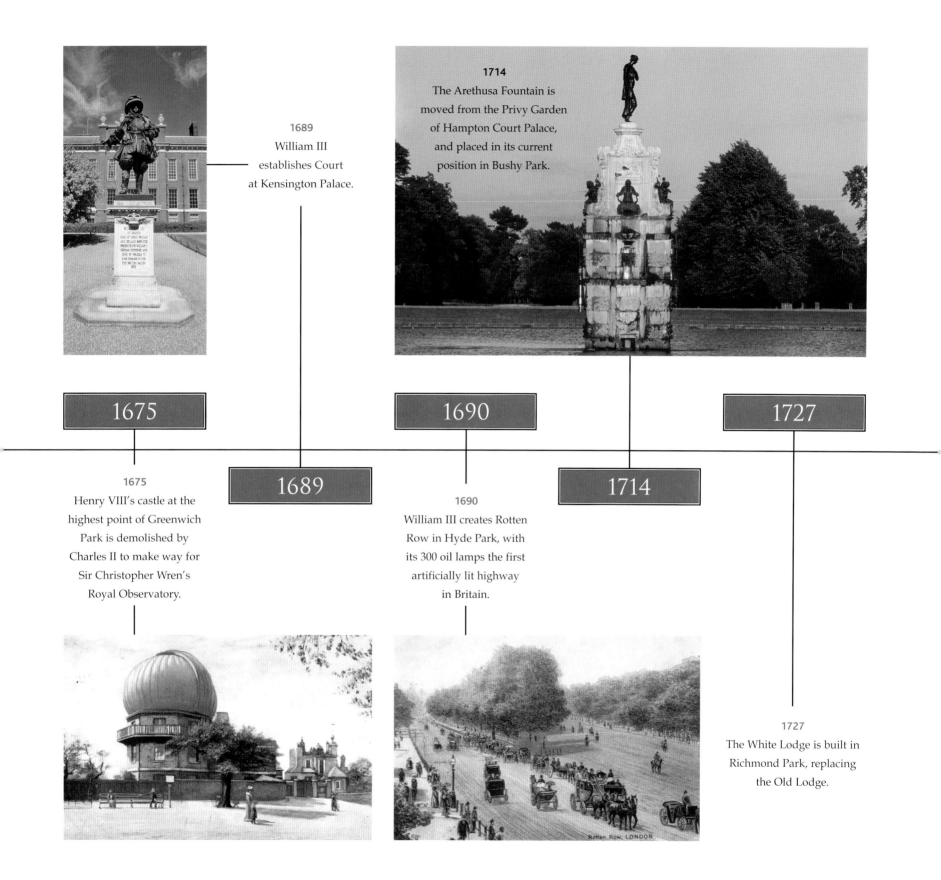

1689

William III establishes Court at Kensington Palace.

1714

The Arethusa Fountain is moved from the Privy Garden of Hampton Court Palace, and placed in its current position in Bushy Park.

1675

1690

1727

1675

Henry VIII's castle at the highest point of Greenwich Park is demolished by Charles II to make way for Sir Christopher Wren's Royal Observatory.

1689

1690

William III creates Rotten Row in Hyde Park, with its 300 oil lamps the first artificially lit highway in Britain.

1714

1727

The White Lodge is built in Richmond Park, replacing the Old Lodge.

1797
The Duke of Clarence,
later William IV, becomes
ranger of Bushy Park,
and lets land there
to tenant farmers.

1749

1771

1730

1749
A fireworks display to
celebrate the end of the
Austrian War of Succession
goes horribly wrong in Green
Park, and burns down the
magnificent Temple of Peace.

1758

1797

1758
A court case, brought by
Richmond brewer John
Lewis, reopens Richmond
Park for the public.

1771
Prime Minister
Lord North moves
into Bushy House, and
his wife becomes
ranger of the park.

1730
The Serpentine is
created in Hyde Park by
Queen Caroline from local
springs and by damming the
waters of the Westbourne, a
tributary of the Thames.

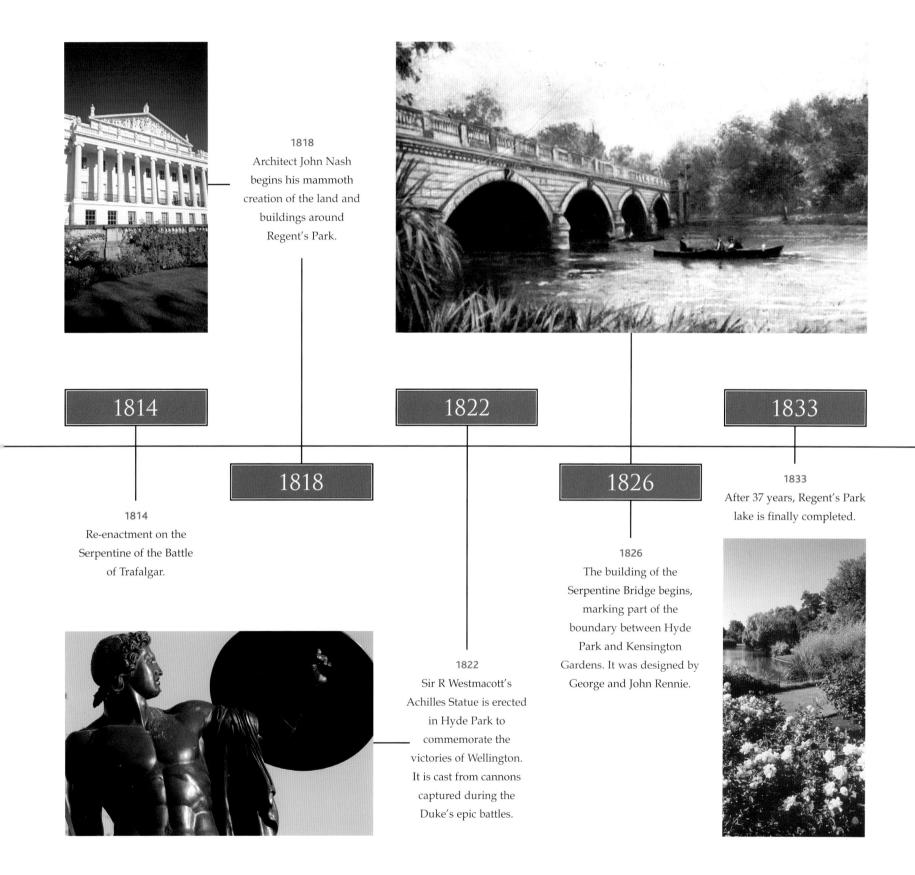

1818
Architect John Nash begins his mammoth creation of the land and buildings around Regent's Park.

1814

1818

1822

1833

1814
Re-enactment on the Serpentine of the Battle of Trafalgar.

1833
After 37 years, Regent's Park lake is finally completed.

1826
The building of the Serpentine Bridge begins, marking part of the boundary between Hyde Park and Kensington Gardens. It was designed by George and John Rennie.

1822
Sir R Westmacott's Achilles Statue is erected in Hyde Park to commemorate the victories of Wellington. It is cast from cannons captured during the Duke's epic battles.

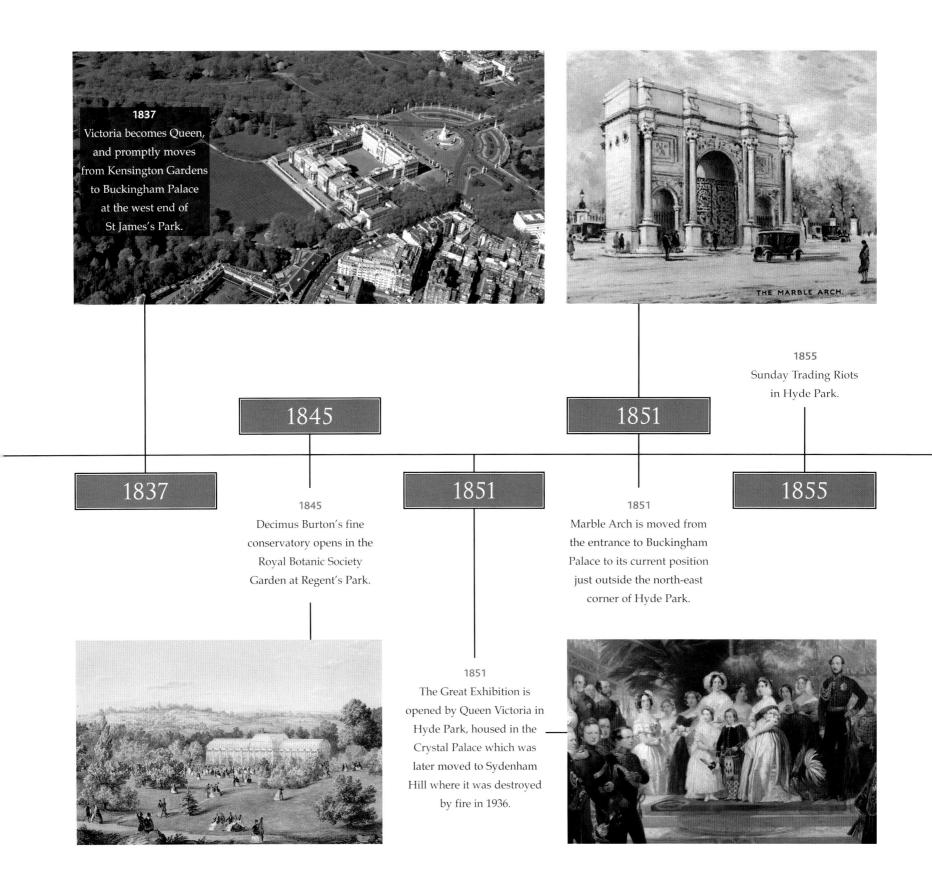

1837
Victoria becomes Queen, and promptly moves from Kensington Gardens to Buckingham Palace at the west end of St James's Park.

THE MARBLE ARCH.

1855
Sunday Trading Riots in Hyde Park.

1845

1851

1837

1851

1855

1845
Decimus Burton's fine conservatory opens in the Royal Botanic Society Garden at Regent's Park.

1851
Marble Arch is moved from the entrance to Buckingham Palace to its current position just outside the north-east corner of Hyde Park.

1851
The Great Exhibition is opened by Queen Victoria in Hyde Park, housed in the Crystal Palace which was later moved to Sydenham Hill where it was destroyed by fire in 1936.

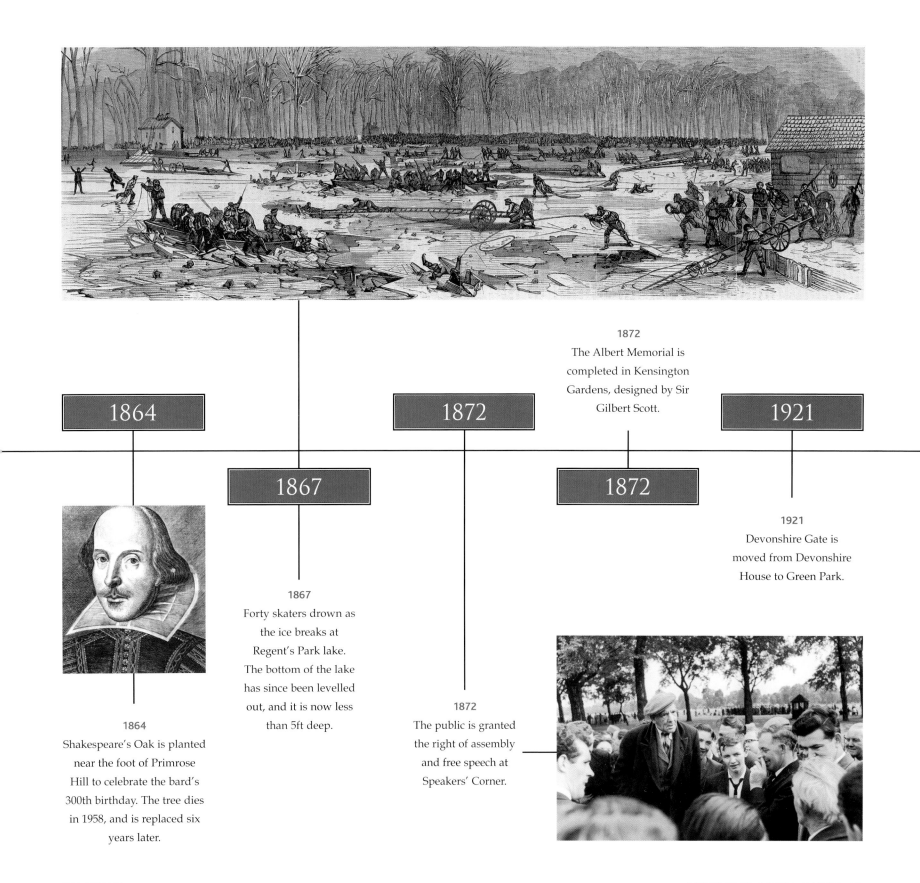

1864

1872

1872
The Albert Memorial is completed in Kensington Gardens, designed by Sir Gilbert Scott.

1921

1867

1872

1921
Devonshire Gate is moved from Devonshire House to Green Park.

1867
Forty skaters drown as the ice breaks at Regent's Park lake. The bottom of the lake has since been levelled out, and it is now less than 5ft deep.

1864
Shakespeare's Oak is planted near the foot of Primrose Hill to celebrate the bard's 300th birthday. The tree dies in 1958, and is replaced six years later.

1872
The public is granted the right of assembly and free speech at Speakers' Corner.

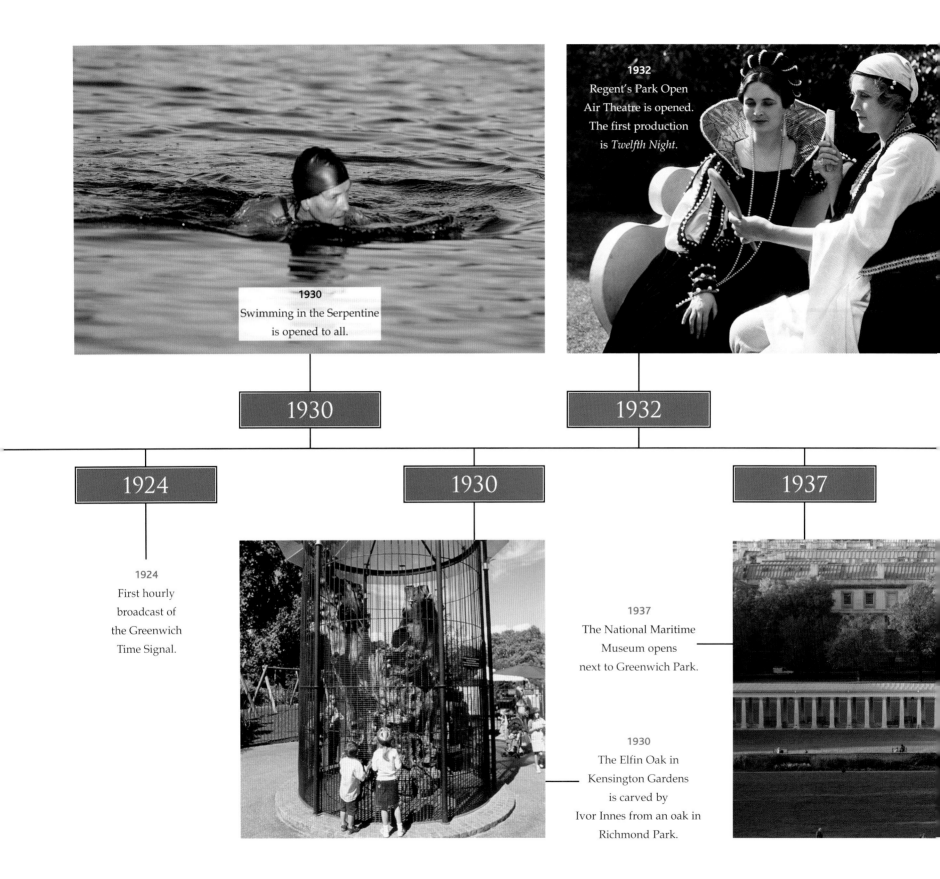

1930
Swimming in the Serpentine
is opened to all.

1932
Regent's Park Open
Air Theatre is opened.
The first production
is *Twelfth Night*.

1930

1932

1924

1930

1937

1924

First hourly
broadcast of
the Greenwich
Time Signal.

1937

The National Maritime
Museum opens
next to Greenwich Park.

1930

The Elfin Oak in
Kensington Gardens
is carved by
Ivor Innes from an oak in
Richmond Park.

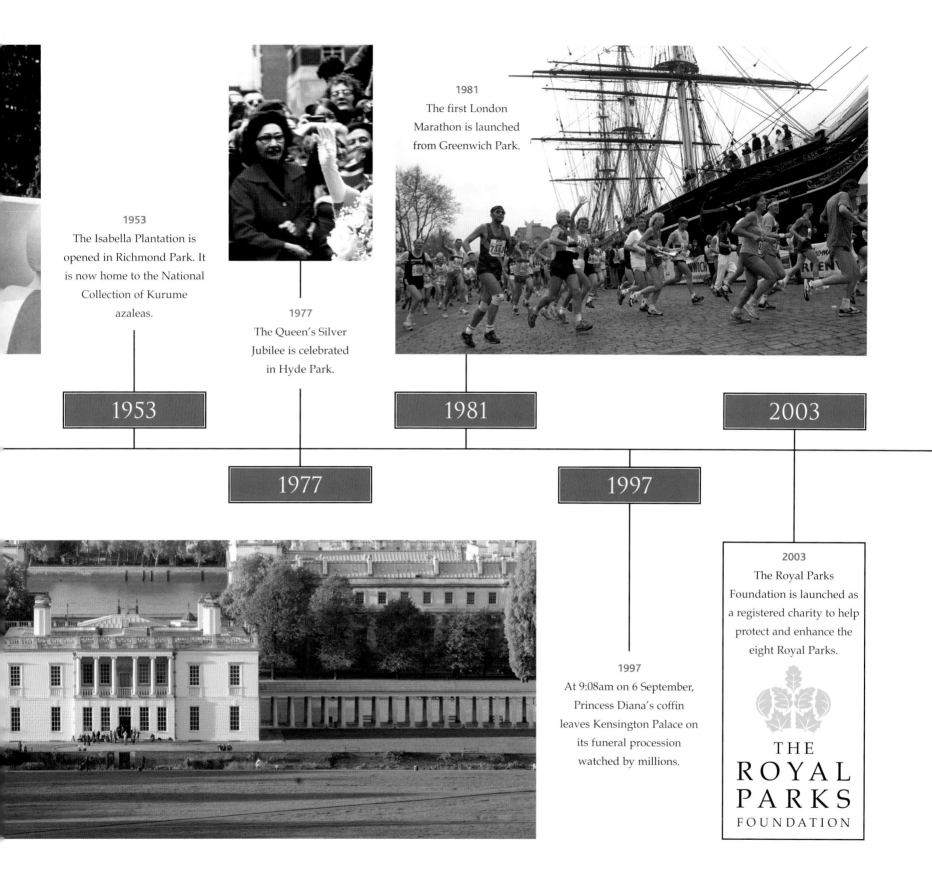

1953
The Isabella Plantation is opened in Richmond Park. It is now home to the National Collection of Kurume azaleas.

1977
The Queen's Silver Jubilee is celebrated in Hyde Park.

1981
The first London Marathon is launched from Greenwich Park.

1997
At 9:08am on 6 September, Princess Diana's coffin leaves Kensington Palace on its funeral procession watched by millions.

2003
The Royal Parks Foundation is launched as a registered charity to help protect and enhance the eight Royal Parks.

THE ROYAL PARKS FOUNDATION

1953

1977

1981

1997

2003

St James's Park

'That green neat lawn and noble timber,

and beyond the dense foliage the grey towers of the Abbey,

and the gold of those Houses of Parliament,

which, despite captious criticism, will always be regarded as the

most splendid examples of the architecture of the

great Victorian era, and close at hand the paths and the parterres,

cause the majesty and greatness of England to

blend with this beautiful oasis islanded between the deserts

of Westminster and Pimlico.'

WS GILBERT, ON ST JAMES'S PARK, 1870

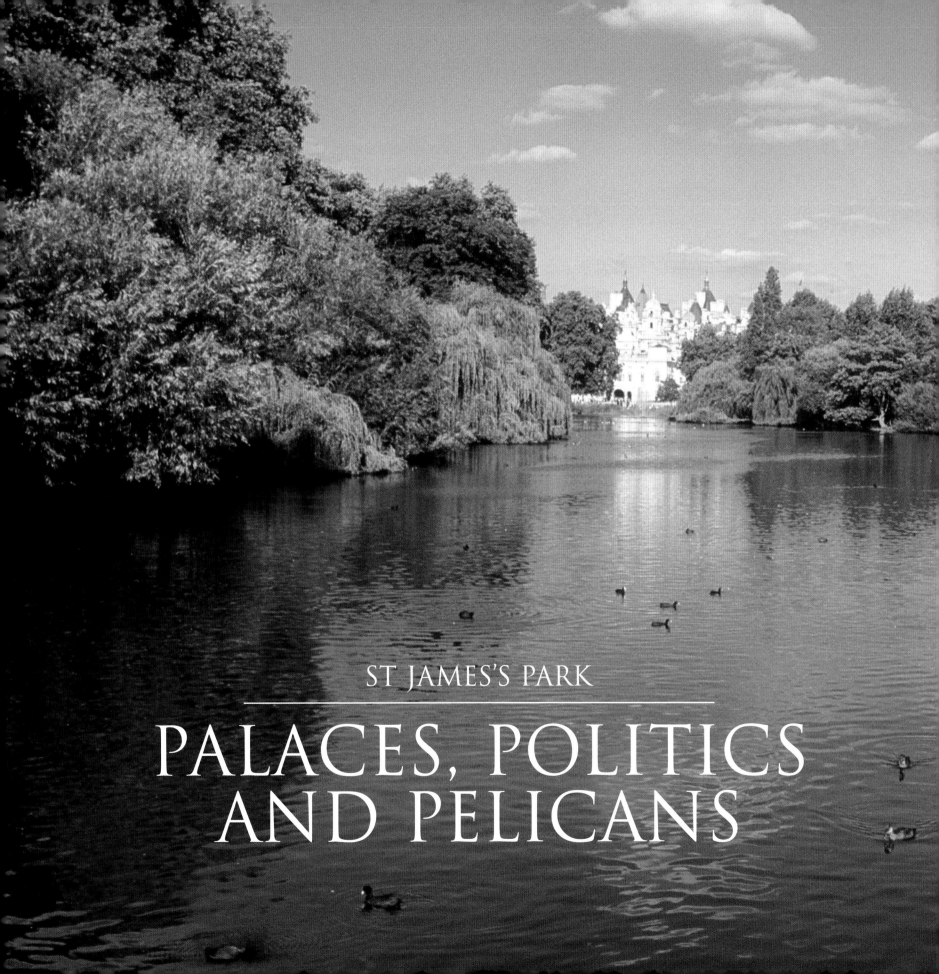

ST JAMES'S PARK

PALACES, POLITICS
AND PELICANS

PALACES, POLITICS AND PELICANS

A man is standing somewhere in England where he is surrounded by the greatest seats of power the nation has ever known. Now here's a question. What is he wearing on his feet?

The answer: wellington boots. The reason: he's standing right in the middle of a duck-pond.

His name was entered at the Horse Guards as an applicant for an ensign's commission; the purchase-money was deposited at an agent's; and Richard, in his usual characteristic way, plunged into a violent course of military study and got up at five o'clock every morning to practise the broadsword exercise.

CHARLES DICKENS

BARNABY RUDGE

Officially, it's more of a lake than a pond, but St James's Lake, home to a great variety of wildfowl and water birds, lies right at the centre of the most awe-inspiring collection of power bases anywhere in the world. If our 'man in the pond' (who we hope has actually had the good sense to stand on the bridge that straddles the water) begins his day by looking to the east and south-east, he will see the sun rise over the twin stations of democratic decision-making, Downing Street and the Houses of Parliament. As the day progresses, he can follow the sun across the sky until it sinks in the west and north-west beyond the old seats of regal power, the great palaces of Buckingham and St James. The old and the new glare at each across an expanse of about 1,000m, separated only by the flower beds, lake, trees, bandstand and winding paths of St James's Park, the oldest of all London's Royal Parks.

All in all, a pretty impressive positioning for a patch of land that was once deemed uninhabitable by all save a dozen or so female lepers and the nuns who looked after them. The tiny colony lived there in the thirteenth century when the Tyburn, which ran from the hills of Hampstead to join the Thames at Vauxhall, and which frequently burst its banks, created a zone so swampy that no one else wanted it. Land in London steadily rose in premium over the years, however, and by the time Henry VIII arrived on the throne he was looking for somewhere new to live. He claimed the patch for himself, drained it, and by the middle of the sixteenth century, the Tyburn had become an underground stream, the King had a deer park to hunt in and a palace to live in, and the leper hospital was long gone… but not forgotten. Run as it had been by the Sisters of St James, the name had stuck.

Animal magic

Hunting remained the principal pursuit until the seventeenth century when James I, a great lover of slaughtering animals in the chase, and of zoos to boot, drained the land further and installed a series of beasts from around the world in a menagerie of his own in the park.

Perhaps the crowning jewels of this collection were the gift of an elephant and five camels from the King of Spain, which caused an uproar in the streets of London as they were marched to the park from their embarkation from the Thames. James was unimpressed with the attention this carnival of the animals created, the beasts being for his private viewing only, so a message was quickly put out: 'that the elephant is to be daily well dressed and fed, but that he should not be led forth to water, nor any admitted to see him, without directions from his keeper, which they were to observe and follow in all things concerning that beast, as they will answer for the contrary at their uttermost peril. The camels are to be daily grazed in the park, but brought back at night, with all possible precautions to screen them from the vulgar gaze.'

St James's Park and its denizens, human and animal, were still for the royal eye only, and may have remained so for

some time, had Oliver Cromwell not interrupted the chain of regal ascent for 11 years. When Charles II resumed the Stuarts' stewardship of national rule in 1660, he set about reforming the park both visually and socially. While exiled in France, he had picked up a few gardening tips from the Palace of Versailles, and upon his return had the park redesigned with avenues of trees, lawns and an ornamental canal. Having created his own personal paradise, he then wanted someone to share it with… so he threw it open to the public.

One member of this public, who lived in Whitehall and spent plenty of time in the newly opened park, was Samuel Pepys. As his diary records, the king was quite frequently seen in St James's mingling with his subjects: 'And so walked to White Hall, an hour or two in the Park, which is now very pleasant. Here the King and Duke [of York] came to see their fowl play. The Duke took very civil notice of me.' [16 March 1662]

It was from this time that many of the park's best-known features began to appear. While in France, the King had enjoyed many a match of a croquet-styled game called paille-maille: Pall Mall and the Mall owe their etymology to his

devotion to the game in his own grounds. Duck Island, home to wildfowl collections from around the world, was created in 1665, (complete with the title of Governor - a human, not avian post), and is still home to many water birds, not least the famous pelicans, first donated to Charles by a Russian ambassador in 1664. A tradition was begun, and for many years pelicans were an ambassadorial gift to the Royal Court of St James.

Guards of honour

Charles still had another development to make at St James's Park, however, but this was not of a civilian nature. When he went into exile after the Battle of Worcester in 1652, he took with him 80 royalist mounted bodyguards. Upon his return, he restructured the parliamentarian Horse Guards using some of his loyal officers, and mustered his new Life Guards at the east end of the park. In later years, this was formally paved over and turned into Horse Guards Parade, where all the king's horses and all the king's men would gather in defence of the realm. More latterly it became the scene of Trooping the Colour, various wartime souvenirs such as a Turkish gun and the Cadiz Memorial set on a cast-iron Chinese dragon… and even a one-time car park for civil servants.

So I to the Park, and there to walk an hour or two; and in the King's garden, and saw the Queen and ladies walk, and there I did steal some apples off the trees.

SAMUEL PEPYS

DIARY

The civil servants apart, Old Henry would have been pleased: in his day, the site had been used for military tournaments. Further changes occurred steadily over the next century and a half, but little to significantly alter the tone and aspect of the park. A tea house was built to provide refreshments to the public: today, Inn The Park is one of the latest incarnations of such a watering hole. In 1711, just to the north of the Mall, Sir Christopher Wren built Marlborough House for the Duchess of that name (it later became the office of the Commonwealth Secretariat). Piece by piece the park was developing without effecting much change.

With one exception. John Sheffield had had a chequered career through the latter half of the seventeenth century, thanks to a remarkable talent for upsetting just about everybody he met. A naval man, he had been sent in 1680 to relieve the town of Tangier, but given command by still unknown enemies of a rotten boat in the hope he wouldn't return; he had been dismissed from court for his overtures to Princess Anne; he was, under James II, made a member of the Privy Council, and dismissed from it later for his anti-William sentiments. Yet he bounced back once more upon the ascension of his beloved Anne to the throne, rapidly became Lord Privy Seal, and was awarded the title Duke of Buckingham. That could have been the end of the story, except that this outspoken individual, who upset many with his poetry and anti-establishment satires (for some of which Dryden was blamed), couldn't resist getting under the skin of just one more person.

Buckingham bucks the trend

At the beginning of the eighteenth century, he decided he wanted a town house in a prominent London spot, and promptly had one built in 1703 in the western corner of St James's Park. His benefactor, Queen Anne, was most upset. The entire aspect of her royal park had suddenly shifted from her northern outlook to a western focal point. The Mall now led up to this new house, the gardens seemed to stretch away from it, and she in her palace appeared to have been shoved off to the side. And worst of all, there was nothing she could do about it.

Decades passed, as did both Anne and the Duke, and in 1761 George III, similarly irritated by the magnificent placement of Buckingham House, bought the thing and had done with it.

His son, George IV, had it converted to a palace, and when Victoria ascended the throne in 1837, she moved her family there lock, stock and barrel, and Buckingham Palace has been the first London home of the royal family ever since.

Just prior to the Victorian era, however, came a further twist in the tale of St James's Park in the form of architect John Nash, whose fortunes can be found in the chapter on Regent's Park with which he is most closely associated. George IV hired him to give the gardens an overhaul, which he did in 1828, in what had become known as the English style. This was based on the inspiration of Humphrey Repton, a Norfolk-born landscape gardener who in the late eighteenth century had softened the old continental style of rigid formality in gardens across the country from Yorkshire to Devon. Although more of an architect, Nash adopted Repton's approach and provided St James's Park with the gentle contours, less formal gardens, and more natural copses that it still enjoys today.

This more restful approach to garden design drew in the public in their hordes, and the park became a true psychological haven for Londoners through the Victorian era. And not just Londoners, either. The French critic, philosopher and historian Hippolyte Taine, recalled in his book *Notes on England* his 1871 visit to the park: 'The things which please me most are the trees. Every day, after leaving the Athenaeum, I go and sit for an hour in St. James's Park; the lake shines softly beneath its misty covering, while the dense foliage bends over the still waters. The rounded trees, the great green domes, make a kind of architecture far more delicate than the other. The eye reposes itself upon these softened forms, upon these subdued tones. These are beauties, but tender and touching, those of foggy countries, of Holland.'

Duck tales

As well as the public, the wildfowl were now in full force in the park. The year 1837 had seen the presentation of a collection of birds to the park – in addition to those it already had – by the Ornithological Society of London, as well as a cottage for a bird-keeper to look after them (a post that still exists today). The writer WS Gilbert was one of many who found them of interest, writing in 1870: 'You go leisurely along, having adjusted your watch by the Horse Guards, looking at the soldiers, and the nurses, and the children, glancing at the island, and looking at the ducks – the dainty, overfed ducks – suggesting all sorts of ornithological lore, not to mention low materialistic associations of green peas or sage and onions. Those dissipated London ducks lay their heads under their

The children were sitting on a seat in St James's Park. They had been watching the pelican repulsing with careful dignity the advances of the seagulls who are always so anxious to play games with it. The pelican thinks, very properly, that it hasn't the figure for games, so it spends most of its time pretending that that is not the reason why it won't play.

E NESBIT

THE STORY OF THE AMULET

The next day I dressed up again, but in quite different clothes, and walked the same way again, but nothing offered till I came into St. James's Park, where I saw abundance of fine ladies in the Park, walking in the Mall, and among the rest there was a little miss, a young lady of about twelve or thirteen years old, and she had a sister, as I suppose it was, with her, that might be about nine years old. I observed the biggest had a fine gold watch on, and a good necklace of pearl, and they had a footman in livery with them; but as it is not usual for the footman to go behind the ladies in the Mall, so I observed the footman stopped at their going into the Mall, and the biggest of the sisters spoke to him, which I perceived was to bid him be just there when they came back.

DANIEL DEFOE

THE FORTUNES & MISFORTUNES OF
THE FAMOUS MOLL FLANDERS

wings and go to roost at quite fashionable hours, that would astonish their primitive country brethren. I hope you like to feed ducks, my friends. All great, good-natured people have a "sneaking kindness" for feeding ducks. There is a most learned and sagacious bishop who won't often show himself to human bipeds, but he may be observed by them in his grounds feeding ducks while philosophising on things in general.'

A park for all people

The park had truly become, to use Gilbert's phrase, one of the 'lungs of London'. Anyone who was anyone visited it, as did anyone who wasn't. They were all catered for, too. 'One of the oddest sights in London,' wrote Charles Dickens' son (also called Charles) in his 1879 *Dictionary of London*, 'is afforded by the colony of gingerbread and sweetstuff stalls in the north-east corner of [St James's] park, at the back of Carlton House Terrace. There is a large consumption of curds and whey, and of milk fresh from the cow, at these primitive restaurants, and the cows which are tethered to the stalls give an air of reality to the promises of their proprietors.'

These were not the only promises on offer, either. The mainly male visitors to St James's, escaping their governmental offices or bored by their cigar-filled clubs that ringed the park, were not averse to a little female company on their strolls, and prostitution, which hit a high in the Victorian era, thrived there. This was nothing new. The park had long been home to the trade in carnal pleasures, illicit affairs and clandestine meetings, much restoration theatre and poetry having focused on it. But as William Congreve noted in the title of his 1700 play partly set in St James's Park, such relationships were 'The Way of the World'.

By the beginning of the twentieth century, however, the world was not in a very good way at all. Early rumblings across the Channel continued to grow into the second decade, and the countless lives that were lost and affected by the four-year devastation visited upon Europe from 1914 to 1918 reshaped societies across the continent as never before. There was little that escaped the deprivations of the period, and St James's Park was no exception. While battle was being waged, its lake was drained, and staff from the nearby government departments overflowed into offices set up along its dry bed.

St James's Park is really, in some ways, quite the prettiest of the London parks, and though sufficiently aristocratic, it is yet much frequented by the populace.

MRS E T COOK

HIGHWAYS & BYWAYS IN LONDON,

1903

The park was restored after the war, and has changed little since. Even the bombs that fell a couple of decades later from Luftwaffe-filled skies failed to affect it, although the adjacent Buckingham Palace was frequently targeted by an enemy bent on demoralisation.

Throughout this time, politicians and officials scurried their way to and fro across the park from palace to Downing Street, Whitehall to Westminster Abbey. In the twentieth century, just as it had been throughout its history, St James's Park was the oasis of calm lying between the power houses of Britain. And still the ducks swam on, just as they have done for centuries, and as they will continue to do.

Today, the park is a magnet for the many visitors who enjoy its rich pageantry, such as Trooping the Colour. But perhaps the last word on St James's Park and its unique embodiment of the contrast yet interdependency between power and peace,

should come from one of the few men who best understood such a delicate balance. The 40-year-old Winston Churchill, then First Lord of the Admiralty, came to the park often during the build-up to WWI, sitting by the lake to think through the issues of the day. On one such occasion he summed up his feelings in a letter to his wife, Clementine.

'My darling one and beautiful,' he wrote. 'Everything tends towards catastrophe and collapse. I am geared up and happy. Is it not horrible to be built like that? The preparations have a hideous fascination for me. I pray to God to forgive me for such fearful moods of levity. Yet I would do my best for peace, and nothing would induce me wrongfully to strike the blow. Two black swans on St. James's Park lake have a darling cygnet – grey, fluffy, precious and unique. I watched them this evening for some time as a relief from all the plans and schemes... Everything is ready as it has never been before. And we are awake to the top of our fingers.'

The Green Park

'Piccadilly does not rank so high in
Clubland, of course, as Pall Mall, but the outlook
over The Green Park – so verdant and
well-timbered – is pleasant in the extreme.'

D LANGE, *THE QUEEN'S LONDON*, 1896

FROM TURBULENCE TO TRANQUILLITY

FROM TURBULENCE TO TRANQUILLITY

New Zealand is one of the most beautiful countries in the world. Boasting a unique flora and fauna, stunning scenery and magnificent open spaces, it's home to a mix of indigenous culture, successful modern business, good food and fine company. Visit it a hundred times, and you'll always find something new.

You'd think, then, that it would stand out as a nation the world would want to visit. But no. To the chagrin of New Zealanders wherever they might go on business or travel, they always find themselves being talked to about somewhere else: their big neighbours to the north-west. 'Ah yes, New Zealand, always meant to go there one day. Been to Australia a couple of times though, now that's a fascinating country.' Still, the New Zealanders aren't all that fussed. They know what the world is missing out on, and that leaves all the more of it for them to enjoy by themselves.

Lovers of London's Green Park could say pretty much the same thing. One of the lesser known parks of London, it has often been ignored by tourists and Londoners alike, who head for St James's Park instead and as a result miss out on its peaceful and simple beauty. The New Zealand to St James's Park's Australia, it sits to the north-west of its historical neighbour, facing the side walls of both Buckingham and St James's Palace, craning its neck to get a view of their front gates. It doesn't have a lake or a parade ground, nor does it back onto Downing Street or Westminster.

In 1842, as if to rub salt into Green Park's wounded pride, *Punch* magazine haughtily exclaimed that it was 'particularly famous for a mud reservoir which adjoins Piccadilly. This elegant stone tank is occasionally filled with water, but is more usually seen applied to its original use, which is to ensure a continual supply of miasmata to the surrounding neighbourhood, and more particularly to the hackney-coach stand which has been humanely placed beside it.'

This rather discomforting sense of the park has also been touched upon in literature. It is rarely used in novels, writers more often sending their characters through St James's or nearby Hyde Park for their plot-progressing perambulations. When it has appeared, however, particularly in the later nineteenth

In April and May, when the trees (always a fortnight earlier than in the country) are vivid on the edge of The Green Park, and the sun has a nearly level ray, there is nothing to equal the smiling loveliness of Piccadilly filled with omnibuses, as seen from the top of the hill, looking east, about Down Street. It is an indescribable scene of streaming colour and gentle variety.

E V LUCAS

A WANDERER IN LONDON, 1906

The Green Park is only separated by an iron railing from the northern side of St. James's Park, and extends westward to Hyde Park Corner, the line of communication being a fine ascent called Constitution Hill. This park adds greatly to the pleasantness both of St James's and Buckingham Palaces, and the line of houses which overlook it on the east.

EDWARD MOGG

NEW PICTURE OF LONDON AND VISITOR'S GUIDE TO ITS SIGHTS, 1844

century and into the early decades of the next, it was often in the context of the seedier, eerier underbelly of life. In Joseph Conrad's *The Secret Agent*, the hollow, lazy, spectral character of the anarchist Yundt is barely revealed, but we do discover that he spends his mornings taking his constitutional walk in Green Park, as if it were the park best suited to his nature. And consider, too, this extract from another novel: 'We walked a little further, and then went in and sat for a while in The Green Park. It was a hot day for autumn, and there was a comfortable seat in a shady place. After a few minutes' staring at nothing, Jonathan's eyes closed, and he went quickly into a sleep, with his head on my shoulder.' The scene sounds innocent enough, except that it is, again, part of a rather disturbing tale. The couple in question are Jonathan Harker and his beloved Mina, part of the gang of vampire hunters in Bram Stoker's *Dracula*.

In short, Green Park has had a bad press, and in the nineteenth century was often portrayed as a park in the shadows of another, with a shadowy nature and where shadowy deeds took place. Given the park's rich history, how could it have become so temporarily unfashionable?

To uncover its history as a Royal Park, we have to go back to the Restoration when Charles II, having returned to the

monarchy from his exile abroad, converted this former meadowland to boost his acreage. He wanted to form a chain of greenery from Bayswater and Kensington at the western reaches of Hyde Park right through to the eastern boundary of St James's Park at Westminster. Upper St James's Park, as it was initially known, provided the king with an enjoyable walk from the palace to Hyde Park Corner, and his constitutional wanderings up the slope eventually provided the route with the name Constitution Hill.

There is a tale from this era – probably apocryphal - which helps to explain the greenness of the park. Charles's wife Catherine, it is said, caught sight of her husband one day picking flowers inside the park, and assumed the appropriate bouquet would shortly be coming her way. Nothing arrived, and when she discovered the nosegay was not for her but her husband's mistress, she ordered the uprooting of every single flower in the park.

Cold comfort

Before long, Charles had doubled the size of the park by adding the land south of the Hill (this is now the gardens behind Buckingham Palace, and closed to the public), and begun to develop his new estate. Although British weather was not as clement as that of southern Europe, he had had two buildings designed which revealed the Mediterranean influence he had picked up on the continent. The Snow House and the Ice House provided cool drinks and refreshments during the summer months, and on the hotter days were the king's favourite hangouts as he picnicked with his courtiers in the grounds.

The eighteenth century saw even further innovations to the park as it rose steadily in monarchic repute. Queen Caroline, George II's wife, was one of the most powerful queens by marriage that Britain had ever had, a popular satiric verse of the 1720s running: 'You may strut, dapper George, but 'twill all be in vain, We all know 'tis Queen Caroline, not you, that reign.' An intelligent, well-educated woman who easily outshone her husband in character and wit, she enjoyed a good intellectual relationship with prime minister Robert Walpole, and as 'Guardian of the Kingdom of Great Britain, and His Majesty's Lieutenant within the same during His

Majesty's absence' was effectively the country's regent during George's frequent excursions to Hanover.

She was especially fond of Upper St James's Park, and set about making some improvements. She had a reservoir – the Queen's Basin – created to supply water to St James's and Buckingham Palace, a pavilion built called the Queen's Library, and continuing the theme, a sunken promenade along the east side of the park which bore the name Queen's Walk. The river Tyburn which had once flowed through the park, was by now covered over by this walk, but Caroline had the Tyburn Pool constructed to enable her to enjoy its waters.

Peak of its powers
By the 1730s, the park was becoming the fashionable new venue for those members of high society who were looking for an alternative to St James's Park. Respect for Caroline was high and, even after her death in 1737, the park remained for a few more years the place to see and be seen.

It was by now the 1740s, and the park had reached its zenith of popularity. It was in the same decade, however, that its star was to begin rapidly to fade.

In 1746, to recognise the park as being independent in its own right, George had it renamed. No longer just a northern version of St James's Park, and with a personality of its own, it was retitled The Green Park (still its official title today, although the definite article is rarely used). These were troubled times in Europe, however, the Austrian war of succession having raged since the beginning of the decade. George, of Hanoverian descent, had got himself involved, hoping to keep his family's homelands free of French invasion, and even becoming the last British king personally to lead his troops into battle. The French, meanwhile, had encouraged the Catholic Jacobites, still smouldering from the severance of their right to the throne in the previous century, to give George something to think about at home. The Battle of Culloden in 1746 was their final attempt at an overthrow, but George's troops won the day. Two years later, the war in Europe was won, too.

So delighted was George with his victorious part in the war both at home and abroad, that he decided to throw a massive party. Commissioning the composer George Frideric Handel, who had written 'Zadok the Priest' for the king's own coronation, to write new music for the celebration, he

She followed them into St. James's Park, and thence (along the Mall) into The Green Park, venturing closer and closer as they reached the grass and ascended the rising ground in the direction of Hyde Park Corner. Her eager eyes devoured every detail in Norah's dress, and detected the slightest change that had taken place in her figure and her bearing. She had become thinner since the autumn – her head drooped a little; she walked wearily. Her mourning dress, worn with the modest grace and neatness which no misfortune could take from her, was suited to her altered station; her black gown was made of stuff; her black shawl and bonnet were of the plainest and cheapest kind. The two little girls, walking on either side of her, were dressed in silk. Magdalen instinctively hated them.

WILKIE COLLINS

NO NAME

announced that the ending of war in Europe would be celebrated in the latest park of choice, the newly renamed Green Park. He had a massive new building constructed to mark the occasion, too, the grandly titled Temple of Peace. It should have gone so well. Handel came up with one of his finest works, Music for the Royal Fireworks, (in fact, 12,000 had come to the rehearsal of the new orchestral work a few days previously, paying 2s 6d per head, and causing a three-hour traffic jam of carriages over London Bridge), and the band, positioned on boats in the Thames, began to play.

Not for long, however. A stray rocket overshot its mark during the performance, and struck the Temple of Peace, which was housing a further 10,000 fireworks. The explosion killed three party-goers, and injured hundreds more, and while the fireworks master and the architect of the building raised their fists to each other, the Temple of Peace was razed to the ground.

The one hundred years woe

Thus began the century of misfortune for Green Park. And what a century of woe it was. Lightning might not strike in the same place twice, but fireworks were to prove they have no such compunction. In 1814, at a gala for the Prince Regent, another huge building, the Temple of Concord, built to commemorate 100 years of Hanoverian rule, was burnt to the ground in an identical manner.

By this time, the park had been sliced in half once more. The land south of Constitution Hill had been appropriated by George III when he took over Buckingham Palace, and turned into the new residence's private gardens. Green Park had become tiny once more, and consequently of less importance to the nobility.

Where recently it was the place to see and be seen, it was rapidly becoming the place to fight and be fought. Before Charles II had appropriated the land, the area had been a popular venue for duellists, and in the eighteenth century this pastime of honour returned. In 1771 the poet Alfieri was challenged to a duel there by Viscount Ligonier, the husband of his mistress. He lost, but despite his injuries, still managed to get back to the Haymarket Theatre in time to see the last act of a play he wanted to see.

Not all duels had such light-hearted endings, however, and as the century rolled over, and attracted by the foolhardy dandies who were so happy to give their lives away, highwaymen were also haunting the park. Eventually, in 1826, Green Park had developed a reputation for danger, and was thrown open to the public by a monarchy that was losing interest in it.

Victoria's ascension to the throne in 1837 did little to alter the park's fortunes. Her move into Buckingham Palace assured that St James's Park, which stretched out in front of her new home, was once again the local Royal Park of attention. The Green Park, off to one side, began literally to fade from view.

Constitution Hill was once more the southern boundary of the park, and Victoria used it frequently for her carriage journeys up towards Hyde Park Corner. Unfortunately for her, this route was no longer quite as safe as it had once been. Not one, not two, but three assassination attempts were made upon her life at the Hill in the 1840s. Perhaps partly in retaliation, perhaps partly because Green Park was not the site where the monarch wanted to spend her money any more, she had those remaining buildings that had not been

destroyed by fireworks – the Queen's Basin and Library, the Ranger's Lodge and the Tyburn Pool – demolished. Green Park was effectively now just grass and trees, and although the Snow House and the Ice House remained, even they were gone by the turn of the twentieth century.

The final event in this century of disaster occurred on 29 June 1850, when former prime minister Robert Peel was out taking a ride up Constitution Hill on his horse. Thrown from its back, he landed badly, and died three days later of his injuries.

In just 101 years, Green Park had lost almost all its buildings, its amenities and half its land, and been the scene of death, robbery and attempted murder. It was little wonder, then, that writers started using it as they did for their scenes of doom and despondency.

Back to nature

But time is a great healer, and so is nature. Left to their own devices, the magnificent trees of Green Park slowly began to dominate the scene; by the beginning of the twentieth century, lime, London plane and hawthorn were all asserting themselves along the paths of this by now so quiet park. As

the years rolled by, so the trees continued to grow, and were enhanced by new plantings of a holly hedge along Piccadilly, and a beech hedge alongside the Queen's Walk, while the central Broad Walk that runs through the park was also developed. Flowers remained at a minimum, bar 250,000 daffodils, specially planted for the Royal Golden Wedding anniversary in 1997. Other than the placing on Piccadilly of the Devonshire Gate, buildings too are at a minimum.

Today, Green Park is a park of arboreal peace, little remaining to record its turbulent history other than the tall leafy sentinels who watched all those kings and queens come and go. Rather symbolically, one tree that was planted to commemorate the coronation of George V has grown so much that its original plaque is now virtually completely covered over with bark. As you sit in the park on a quiet day, your peace interrupted by the occasional jogger taking their

lunchtime break, or a squirrel nosing around your feet for the possible tasty offerings that you might have dropped, or the wind rippling through the leaves of the trees above your head, close your eyes, and you may hear a faint noise. To some, it's the sound of centuries past, of firework displays and regal parties, of musical extravaganzas and crowds yelling on duellists, of rolling carriages and shadowy deeds.

In reality, it is a sound older than all of these, a truly ancient rumble. What you are listening to is the flow of the River Tyburn, still just detectable, as it trundles its way south beneath your feet, passing by on its way to the Thames. As it flows past, like so many of the tourists to London, with nary a glance at the park in which you sit, you sense that you have found one of the true gentle jewels in London's crown, and that if the world wishes to hurry on by without pausing a while, then that's the world's loss, not yours.

Hyde Park

'The degree of freedom of the press existing in this
country is often over-rated. Technically there is great freedom,
but the fact that most of the press is owned
by a few people operates in much the same way as State censorship.
On the other hand, freedom of speech is real.
On a platform, or in certain recognised open air spaces
like Hyde Park, you can say almost anything.'

GEORGE ORWELL, 1945

HYDE PARK

FROM MONKS
TO MARX

FROM MONKS TO MARX

*Rotten Row means 'Route de Roi',
or the King's Way, but now it's more
like a riding school than anything
else. The horses are splendid, and the
men, especially the grooms, ride well,
but the women are stiff, and bounce,
which isn't according to our rules.
I longed to show them a tearing
American gallop, for they trotted
solemnly up and down, in their
scant habits and high hats, looking
like the women in a toy Noah's Ark.
Everyone rides – old men, stout
ladies, little children – and the young
folks do a deal of flirting here. I
saw a pair exchange rose buds, for
it's the thing to wear one in the
button-hole, and I thought it rather
a nice little idea.*

LOUISA MAY ALCOTT

LITTLE WOMEN

'[The] alliance between a degenerate, dissipated and pleasure-seeking aristocracy and the Church – built on a foundation of filthy and calculated profiteering on the part of the beer magnates and monopolistic wholesalers gave rise to a mass demonstration in Hyde Park yesterday, such as London has not seen since the death of George IV, the "first gentleman of Europe". We witnessed the event from beginning to end and believe we can state without exaggeration that yesterday in Hyde Park the English revolution began.'

The date that this article was written for the German publication *Neue Oder-Zeitung* was 25 June, 1855. The writer had witnessed first hand what were to become known as the 'Sunday Trading Riots', an outbreak of demonstration and violence by the working classes of London in response to the government's new bill to ban most Sunday trading as a mark of respect for the Church. As many working people got paid on Saturday and therefore only had Sundays in which to make their purchases, they felt this was an unfair collusion against them by Church and State combined.

The writer of the article was with them all the way. He was Karl Marx, whose own work was to inspire future generations of revolutionaries in the decades ahead against domination by Church and State. But in the heat of the moment, was he being overly romantic to describe Hyde Park as the venue of the beginning of the English revolution?

Perhaps not. The history of Hyde Park is an almost textbook summary of the progression of land ownership and social freedoms in English history, and the struggles that have punctuated it. A focal point of the Roman and Norman eras, it evolved into an agricultural haven for monks, a happy hunting ground for the monarchy, and a forum for reformists of political structures. Anyone who wants a quick overview of this nation's history could do worse than study the changing fortunes of the patch of land today called Hyde Park.

Ancient history

The parish, or manor, itself has been known as Hyde since at least the Domesday book, when its heavily wooded areas stretched across a 'hyde', probably a measure of between 80 and 120 acres. Such fine hunting land was it that King William donated it to one of his favourites, Geoffrey de Mandeville, in return for his services in the overthrow of Harold in 1066. Upon his death, de Mandeville bequeathed it to the Benedictine monks of St Peter, Westminster who cleared some of the forest and turned the land over to agriculture, maintaining it in this way for about four and a half centuries.

One of the reasons the land was so prized was its accessibility. A thousand years even before William, the Romans had laid a lattice of roads across the country, two of the most important of which crossed at what is now the north-eastern corner of the park. Watling Street (now Edgware Road and Park Lane) ran north to south, while the Via Trinobatina (now Oxford Street and Bayswater Road) ran east to west. It was well watered, too, the Westbourne and Tyburn streams crossing its acres. If anything, it was amazing that the Benedictines were able to hold on to such prime land for so long.

As was so often the case during his reign, it was Henry VIII who put an end to the monks' ownership, claiming it from them in 1536 for his own hunting purposes, and turning it into a Royal Park. The kings and queens of England proceeded to enjoy the park for the next century, until Charles I finally opened it to the public.

Although several aspects of Hyde Park owe their origin to the monarchy over the years (Rotten Row, for example, is thought to be an Anglicisation of 'Route du Roi'; the Parade Ground is a throw-back to the days when Elizabeth I reviewed her troops there; the Serpentine, named for its sinuous shape, was commissioned by George II's wife, Queen Caroline), it is the role that the park played in the lives of the general public from the seventeenth century onwards which makes it most interesting.

One of the most famous events of that century is a perfect example. The Great Plague, which struck in 1665, was a devastation to London, with so many of its citizens living in such close quarters that the disease spread almost as quickly as the fire that was to strike the following year. In an attempt to escape the ravages of the plague, many Londoners set up camp in the park, hoping that its verdant lands would protect them from the unsanitary conditions of much of the rest of the city that carried the threat of death.

The idea of the park as a sanctuary, as a means of public escape, continued through the eighteenth century and into the nineteenth. Public exhibitions were held there, including in 1814 what must have been an extraordinary celebration

WATER WAYS

VISITORS PADDLE THEIR FEET IN THE PARK'S DIANA MEMORIAL (LEFT), WHILE A CANADA GOOSE TAKES IT EASY (ABOVE)

of the victory at Trafalgar: there were fireworks and even
a re-enactment of the battle, French ships being sunk on
the Serpentine with the national anthem playing in
the background.

Yet even this was to pale beside the venture launched nearly
40 years later which was possibly the greatest public spectacle
that Britain had ever introduced. Prince Albert had long been
impressed by a new approach to industry that was being
employed in France. For some decades, the French had been
advertising their industrial developments to the world in a
series of exhibitions, each of them designed to showcase the
best of business. Today, we've become used to car shows, boat
shows, Ideal Home shows and the like, but when in the mid-
nineteenth century Albert put his proposal to the government
for a Best of British exhibition, to show off the nation's great
strides in art and industry 'for the purposes of exhibition, of
competition and of encouragement', the response was
lukewarm. Such an exhibition, he said, 'would afford a true
test of the point of development at which the whole of
mankind has arrived in this great task, and a new starting
point from which all nations would be able to direct their
further exertions.'

FUN IN THE PARK:
CONCERTS LIKE LIVE 8 THAT TOOK
PLACE IN 2005 MIGHT BE ONE-OFFS
(LEFT), BUT THE SERPENTINE IS THERE
TO ENJOY ALL YEAR ROUND

Although support was slow to come from government, the Society of Arts pitched in to this idea with great enthusiasm, raising funds and generating support. A Royal Commission was reluctantly passed in the House, and eventually an extraordinary £230,000 was raised.

The greatest show on earth

The Great Exhibition was finally unveiled in 1851, Hyde Park as the venue, and housed in a mighty domed structure called the Crystal Palace, designed by the architect Joseph Paxton. So huge was the building, – nearly 2,000ft long, and about six times the area covered by St Paul's Cathedral – that there were fears it might collapse, and before the event was officially opened, hundreds of army sappers and miners were brought in to march up and down to see if their vibrations caused any structural damage. It survived.

The Exhibition was truly one of the greatest public events in British history. As the *Art Journal* recorded at the time, it did far more than just showcase British products; it provided in its series of great halls examples of human endeavour from the full reaches of the British Empire and beyond. It's worth recalling that publication's account of what could be seen on show to get a true impression of how awesome it must have been: 'We have here the Indian Court, Africa, Canada, the West Indies, the Cape of Good Hope, the Medieval Court, and the English Sculpture Court... Birmingham, the great British Furniture Court, Sheffield and its hardware, the woollen and mixed fabrics, shawls, flax, and linens, and printing and dyeing... general hardware, brass and iron-work of all kinds, locks, grates... agricultural machines and implements... the mineral products of England... the cotton fabric and carriage courts, leather, furs, and hair, minerals and machinery, cotton and woollen power-looms in motion... flax, silk, and lace, rope-making lathes, tools and minerals, marine engines, hydraulic presses, steam machinery, Jersey, Ceylon, and Malta with the Fine Arts Court behind them; Persia, Greece, Egypt, and Turkey, Spain, Portugal, Madeira and Italy, France, its tapestry, machinery, arms and instruments, occupying two large courts; Belgium, her furniture, carpets and machinery; Austria, with her gorgeous furniture courts and machinery furniture, North of Germany and Hase Towns; Russia, with its malachite doors, vases and ornaments, and the United States, with its agricultural implements, raw materials etc.

'We pass from the United States to Sweden, part of Russia, Denmark, a division of the Zollverein, Russian cloths, hats and carpets, Prussian fabrics, Saxony, and the Austrian sculpture court, another division of France with its splendid frontage of articles of vertu and ornamental furniture, its magnificent court for plate, bronzes and china; its tasteful furniture, and carpets, its jewels, including those of the Queen of Spain; its laces, gloves and rich embroideries; Switzerland, China and Tunis...

'In the British half are the silks and shawls, lace and embroideries, jewellery and clocks and watches, behind them military arms and models, chemicals, naval architecture, philosophical instruments, civil engineering, musical instruments, anatomical models, glass chandeliers, china, cutlery, and animal and vegetable manufactures, china and pottery... on the opposite side perfumery, toys, fishing materials, wax flowers, stained glass, British, French, Austrian, Belgian, Prussian, Bavarian and American products.'

A staggering total of over six million people visited the Great Exhibition during the five and a half months that it was open, and once it was over, the Crystal Palace was disassembled and rebuilt in Sydenham Park (where it burnt down in 1934). Yet its short tenure had shown to many that Hyde Park had by now become the Royal Park of the people and for the people, as democratic a venue as could be imagined.

STATUESQUE SURROUNDINGS

ACHILLES AT HYDE PARK CORNER (ABOVE, LEFT) IS FLANKED HERE BY BOY AND DOLPHIN (LEFT) AND LITTLE NELL, BOTH OF WHICH CAN BE FOUND IN THE PARK ITSELF

THE MANY FACES OF SPEAKERS'
CORNER, WHICH WAS GRANTED
THE RIGHT OF ASSEMBLY AND FREE
SPEECH IN 1872

It's now

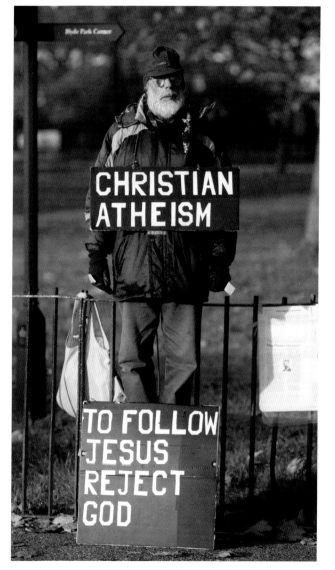

CHRISTIAN ATHEISM

TO FOLLOW JESUS REJECT GOD

And yet true democracy can only exist where there is free speech. The riots that Karl Marx attended only four years after the Great Exhibition, and of which he had such high hopes, were in fact just part of a centuries-long process of liberalisation that was coming to a head. The truly democratic nature of Hyde Park was still just around the corner, and it had its roots not so much in the lives of Londoners, but in their deaths.

Hanging gardens

It was as far back as the twelfth century that the Tyburn that ran across the land of Hyde was first recorded as being the site of a public hanging. On a spot near where Marble Arch stands today, this site rapidly became London's premier execution site, and in 1571 a huge gallows was erected which could hang up to 24 people in one go. The Tyburn Tree, as it was known, became an icon of mixed fascination and fear, public executions attracting thousands on a 'good' day, mothers telling their young that if they didn't behave they'd be 'sent to Tyburn'. Executioners were both entertainers and bogeymen, their monthly duties enthralling and appalling the public in equal measure.

The poet John Taylor neatly summed up the gruesome spectacle:

'I have heard sundry men oft times dispute
Of trees, that in one year will twice bear fruit.
But if a man note Tyburn, t'will appear,
That that's a tree that bears twelve times a year.'

This deadly corner of Hyde Park soon became in the sixteenth century a site of public holidays, Londoners travelling from all over the city to leer at the unfortunates as they dangled from their ropes, and to hear their final words of despair or defiance. The condemned were allowed to address their public before the ropes tautened, many of them aiming their final barbs at the State or Church. The poverty of the working classes was one major theme; opposition to the Church of England by Catholics who had done nothing other than practice their own religion was another. It is said that some people even converted to Catholicism on the basis of dying men's speeches.

Newgate Prison became London's official place of execution in 1759, but the tradition of free speech had become established at Hyde Park, albeit not officially. Hyde Park had become the venue of the 1855 Sunday Trading Riots because of the site's traditions, but the next few years were to bring about a final and dramatic revolution.

Edmund Beales, a middle-class barrister and president of the Workmen's Peace Association, was a great believer that without free speech and suffrage, peace was impossible. In 1866 he led his Reform League to Hyde Park to protest at the lack of a working man's vote, and violence broke out with the police. Others followed. Perhaps it was because the times were changing; perhaps the public nature of the site carried too much weight, but the government decided not to clamp down on this civil disobedience, and in 1872 granted the right of assembly and free speech to this north-eastern corner of Hyde Park, and named it Speakers' Corner.

In the decades that followed, Speakers' Corner became what the internet is today, an outlet for political, religious and moral opinions of every hue. From suffragettes to campaigners for nuclear disarmament, shop-keepers to celebrities, anyone who

He passed into Hyde Park, now silent and deserted, and increased his rate of walking as if in the hope of leaving his thoughts behind.
CHARLES DICKENS
THE LIFE AND ADVENTURES OF NICHOLAS NICKLEBY

wants to broadcast their message to as many as they can, have used this historic site as their soapbox to London. Orwell and Lenin both spoke there as, of course, did Karl Marx.

Hyde Park has continued to enjoy a truly public outlook ever since. The scene of many Parties in the Park, it has housed in the last hundred years or so a pet cemetery, allotments during the World War I's Dig for Victory campaign, and an exhibition to mark the Queen's Silver Jubilee in 1977.

This truly public park is one of the great places to visit in London. You can ride horses there, swim or row in the Serpentine, play tennis, go inline skating, or simply lie on the grass and watch the world getting on with its business. If you close your eyes, you can even imagine it as it once was when times were changing but people were oh so similar.

In his book *Saunterings in and about London*, the writer Max Schlesinger described this great park of British history by discussing the people in it. Schlesinger betrays his own class judgements in the piece, but it's a perfect summary of the nature of Hyde Park, written as it was in 1853.

'Early in the morning the lake is plebeian. The children of the neighbourhood swim their boats on it; apprentices on their way to work make desperate casts for some half-starved gudgeon; the ducks come forward in dirty morning wrappers. Nursery-maids with babies innumerable take walks by order; and at a very early hour a great many plebeians have the impertinence to bathe in the little lake.

'But today the park and the river are in true aristocratic splendour; here and there, there is indeed some stray nursery-maid walking on the grass, and some little tub of a boat with a ragged sail floating on the lake; there is also a group of anglers demonstrating to one another with great patience that the fish won't bite today, but all along the banks of the river far down to the end of the park and up to the majestic shades of Kensington Gardens there is an interminable throng of horses and carriages.'

The 'revolution' was just around the corner.

Kensington Gardens

'[Peter's] age is one week, and though he was
born so long ago he has never had a birthday, nor is there the
slightest chance of his ever having one.
The reason is that he escaped from being a human
when he was seven days' old; he escaped
by the window and flew back to the Kensington Gardens.'

JM BARRIE, *PETER PAN*, 1904

KENSINGTON GARDENS

NEVERLAND

KENSINGTON PALACE

NEVERLAND

It is one of the greatest of human paradoxes that our destinations are often less memorable than the journeys that brought us there. Having striven to arrive at new lands or new stages in life, their lustre eventually begins to wither, and we long for the emotions that carried us there in the first place, for that innocent, enthusiastic glow of anticipation that once drove us on.

For many of us, it is the journey from childhood to adulthood that sometimes gives us pause for nostalgic yearning. We look back upon those early years that shaped us, and smile at the ambitious, wildly creative yet simple dreams we once had. There are moments when we want to combine the impossible, recreating our earlier innocence in a perpetual scenario. Yet we know that we cannot go back, and even if we could, we would be taking our lost innocence with us.

There must have been times during Queen Victoria's long journey through life as Britain's monarch when she would have given anything to go back. The premature death of her beloved Albert famously left her mourning those happier

years for decades, but she had been an unlikely candidate for queen in the first place. Her predecessor, William IV, had no fewer than 12 children, but as 10 of them were illegitimate, and the two that his wife Adelaide bore him died in childhood, he had no heirs upon his death in 1837. Victoria, his niece, was therefore next in line, and was only 18 when she came to the throne.

Such a sharp demarcation between childhood and adulthood is rarely experienced, but Victoria was made of stern stuff. She grew up virtually overnight, leaving behind the dressing-up games, fast horse-riding, pet canaries and naughty behaviour of her youth. She also had to leave behind her home for those first 18 years, Kensington Palace.

If Kensington Palace was the future queen's home, then Kensington Gardens was her playground. The close circle that protected her during her youth ensured that entertainment and visitors rarely came to the palace, so the gardens became her escape. As a small child, she could often be found wandering around the flowerbeds watering the plants – on one occasion missing completely and pouring the water over her shoes. Unaware for many years that she would one day

Personally I would view with composure a veto prohibiting me from all the parks, so long as I might have the freedom of Kensington Gardens. Here one sees the spring come in as surely and sweetly as in any Devonshire lane; here the hawthorns burst into flower as cheerily as in Kent; here is much shade, and chairs beneath it, and cool grass to walk on.

E V LUCAS

A WANDERER IN LONDON, 1906

The birds sing sweetly in these trees

Across the girdling city's hum

MATTHEW ARNOLD

LINES WRITTEN IN

KENSINGTON GARDENS

become queen, she was bemused – and amused – by the many people who bowed and scraped to her as she wandered around the park. Although in later life she was to describe her childhood at Kensington as dull and restricted, it was a time of great innocence, a complete contrast to what was to come in her long life. And Kensington Gardens, the western part of the near-rectangle of land shared with Hyde Park, would always remind her of that innocent childhood.

In that, Queen Victoria was not alone. Virginia Woolf was a great lover of the park, escaping to it whenever she could from the sorrows following the premature death of her mother and the 'respectful mummified humbug' of her upbringing. She spent many happy times there, sailing boats on the Round Pond, hunting for beetles and playing with the shells that constitute the Flower Walk. In *The Years*, she wrote lovingly of the park: 'Not yet trodden down [the leaves] lay in Kensington Gardens, and children, crunching the shells as they ran, scooped up a handful and scudded on through the mist down the avenues, with their hoops.'

Other writers, too, have used the park to throw wistful glances in the direction of innocent childhood. In Thackeray's *Vanity*

PETER PAN STATUE

Fair, we read that: 'On that day, for "business" prevented him on weekdays from taking such a pleasure, it was old Sedley's delight to take out his little grandson Georgy to the neighbouring parks or Kensington Gardens, to see the soldiers or to feed the ducks.' And Wilkie Collins's character Julian Gray, in *The New Magdalen*, states: 'You can't think how pleasant I found the picture presented by the Gardens, as a contrast. The ladies in their rich winter dresses, the smart nursery maids, the lovely children, the ever moving crowd skating on the ice of the Round Pond; it was all so exhilarating after what I have been used to, that I actually caught myself whistling as I walked through the brilliant scene!'

This theme of children at play is perhaps more associated with Kensington Gardens than any of the other Royal Parks. And fittingly so, because it is the youngest of them all, and spent its formative years as part of another park, before attaining independent status in its own right.

The younger years

It was in 1689 that the asthmatic William III decided with his queen, Mary, that it was time to move to a healthier climate than Whitehall. Looking around London, their eye fell upon a

Jacobean mansion owned by the Earl of Nottingham and situated on the west side of Hyde Park. They forked out the near £20,000 asking fee, and hired Sir Christopher Wren to modify it for royal residence. The work was quickly undertaken, Queen Mary taking a keen interest in seeing it completed as soon as possible, and often visiting the site. Leaving the mansion more or less as the core of the new building, Wren simply added a new block to each corner and extended the courtyard.

Kensington House – William and Mary were reluctant to call it a palace – effectively became the monarchs' winter residence and family retreat, and William, who was very fond of art, ensured that his favourite paintings were hung on its walls.

Queens of the gardens

When Queen Anne ascended to the throne in 1702, she decided she wanted to make a little more of her Kensington home. She had the place refurnished, and called Wren back into service to design for her the Orangery in the palace grounds. Appropriating a little more of Hyde Park than her predecessors, she loved her gardens around Kensington Palace, and would often take a turn around them with her

great love, Prince George of Denmark. When George died in 1708, she was so devastated that she was unable to return to Kensington for 18 months, but once mourning was over, she made the palace her home once more, dying there in 1714.

Then came the Georges. The first had the palace modified further, while the third had no interest in the grounds at all. George II, however, had a wife, and it was Queen Caroline who really brought Kensington Gardens to life for the first time.

At the time of Caroline's arrival at Kensington, the gardens took up barely 50 acres of Hyde Park. Under her watchful eye, however, a further 200 acres were claimed, and they were no wasted acquisition. In the late 1720s work began on a redesign, and its results can still be seen today.

This particular Queen Caroline may not have washed her hair in turpentine (that nursery rhyme commemorates George IV's wife from the following century), but she certainly washed Hyde Park with the Serpentine. Damming the River Westbourne, which ran down to the Thames at Chelsea, she created the famous lake that wends its way from Lancaster Gate in the north to Fisherman's Keep towards the

The third day succeeding their knowledge of the particulars, was so fine, so beautiful a Sunday as to draw many to Kensington Gardens, though it was only the second week in March.

JANE AUSTEN

SENSE AND SENSIBILITY

south-eastern corner of the park, and is known in the Kensington Gardens section as the Long Water. Pollution of the Westbourne in the nineteenth century prevented its use any further as a source for the lake, and since 1998 the water has been pumped up from a borehole in Kensington Gardens. It also supplies water to the Gardens' other main focal point, the Round Pond, where children's boats and ducklings have jostled for space for over a century and a half.

Opening times

Framed by the Broad Walk with the palace behind it on the west side, and West Carriage Drive on the east, Kensington Gardens had come of age. Seeing no need to keep its tree-lined splendour and magnificent water features private, George and Caroline opened the park to the public at certain times, with the quaint caveat that they must be 'respectably dressed', and by the time that George III abandoned the palace in 1762 for Buckingham Palace, daily admittance had been introduced.

It was best not to hang around too long, however, as a neat little anonymous verse found attached to one of the park benches in the nineteenth century pointed out:

'Poor Adam and Eve were from Eden turned out,
As a punishment due to their sin;
But here after eight, if you loiter about,
As a punishment you'll be locked in.'

Victoria may have felt locked in at Kensington Palace during her youth, but as Queen she paid Kensington Gardens the deepest respect. Upon her husband's death she had the Albert Memorial built on the park's southern edge, and the Italian Gardens near Lancaster Gate also appeared during her reign.

Kensington Gardens, by now, were no longer a principal royal residence, but as the Victorian era rolled by, they were becoming an increasingly popular family venue for afternoon and evening strolls. The rising middle classes of society were making their homes around Bayswater and Kensington, and while they worked their way further up the social ladder, the park provided their nannied children with the perfect place to play. The late Victorian edict that children should be seen and not heard could be escaped among the elms and beside the

ALBERT MEMORIAL

waters that, as already noted, provided many a writer born in the nineteenth century with happy memories. The novelist, Mary Augusta Ward, who wrote under the name Mrs Humphrey Ward, summed this up perfectly in her novel *A Great Success*. 'After tea [Doris] strolled out into Kensington Gardens, and sat under the shade of trees already autumnal, watching the multitude of children – children of the people – enjoying the nation's park all to themselves, in the complete absence of their social betters. What ducks they were, some of them – the little, grimy, round-faced things – rolling on the grass, or toddling after their sisters and brothers. They turned large, inquisitive eyes upon her, which seemed to tease her heart-strings.'

Elves and fairies

Such a strong literary history would already have given Kensington Gardens its reputation as the children's park. In fact, literature has not been alone in the arts to use these gardens in such a way. When in 1928 the sculptor Ivor Innes began his work transforming an ancient oak tree from Richmond Park into a carved structure of elves, fairies and animals – the Elfin Oak – it was Kensington Gardens to which the tree was removed and placed. Innes and his wife went on to write a book about it, *The Elfin Oak of Kensington Gardens*, and this listed sculpture still stands there today alongside the children's playground, and was a great favourite of the Goon and children's writer, Spike Milligan, who twice raised funds for its restoration.

Yet there is still one final event to recall that carves that childhood role, both figuratively and literally, most completely into the park's history. Mrs Humphrey Ward wrote her novel in 1916, the same year that London first witnessed a new play entitled *A Kiss for Cinderella*. A romance, the play concerns a char-girl who cares for four young orphans, and who finally finds love. *The Times* declared upon seeing it that 'the fairy-tale has entered into the common London world.'

They were not quite right. The author, JM Barrie, had done it once before. Born and educated in Scotland, Barrie had moved to London as a young man, and taken residence near Kensington Gardens where he liked to wander with his dog Porthos and watch the world go by. Among the many children

who played in its grounds, he soon befriended the five young sons of the Llewelyn-Davies family, and through them the parents. He would invent stories and games for them to play, often based on pirates and castaways, and later became their guardian on the deaths of their parents. A man of very short stature, often dressed in an overcoat a size or two too large for him, and shy and anxious about the demands of masculine adult life, Barrie slipped easily into the company of young and imaginative people, counting fictional writers and children among his best friends. His play, *Peter Pan*, which was first shown in 1904, was about the innocence of childhood and the aggression of adulthood, and the refusal to make the transition from one to the other.

It went down a storm, and has done so ever since. The Boy Who Never Grew Up grew into a legend instead, Barrie himself donating a statue of the character to Kensington Gardens where his tale was based. The theme is adored by the young who see it as a paean to themselves, and it is wistfully loved by the old, for whom it has tragic undertones: if Peter Pan could hold on to his youth, fearing not even death itself ('To die,' says Peter 'will be an awfully big adventure'), then why cannot we? We know the answer though, for as Barrie

Mrs Darling loved to have everything just so, and Mr Darling had a passion for being exactly like his neighbours; so, of course, they had a nurse. As they were poor, owing to the amount of milk the children drank, this nurse was a prim Newfoundland dog, called Nana, who had belonged to no one in particular until the Darlings engaged her. She had always thought children important, however, and the Darlings had become acquainted with her in Kensington Gardens, where she spent most of her spare time peeping into perambulators, and was much hated by careless nursemaids, whom she followed to their homes and complained of to their mistresses.

JM BARRIE

PETER PAN

wrote, 'all children, except one, grow up. They soon know that they will grow up, and the way Wendy knew was this. One day when she was two years old she was playing in a garden, and she plucked another flower and ran with it to her mother. I suppose she must have looked rather delightful, for Mrs Darling put her hand to her heart and cried, "Oh, why can't you remain like this for ever!" This was all that passed between them on the subject, but henceforth Wendy knew that she must grow up. You always know after you are two. Two is the beginning of the end.'

This is the great dual nature of Kensington Gardens. It is a playground for the children who know that they will grow up one day, but that this is not that day. It is also a permanent reminder in adulthood that as we outgrow our young lives we can never regain their unknowingness. We can't go back, we have to keep moving forward, and leave children behind in our places to continue the cycle.

Queen Victoria, who could never go back to Kensington Gardens, or to the less burdened days of her youth, did at least mirror Peter Pan in one aspect. There is a statue of her in front of Kensington Palace, looking out across the Broad Walk and the Round Pond where she played as a child. Although it was sculpted to celebrate the first 50 years of her reign, the figure is of a young woman, sitting comfortably upon her new throne, at the threshold of her new adult life. And because this is Kensington Gardens, the park of childhood, in which each generation looks down fondly at the next, there was really only one person who could have put it there.

It was sculpted by Princess Louise, one of Victoria's children.

Regent's Park

'I had had a terrible night. My mind felt much as it had felt on
the evening when I had gone to the play. I went out to see what the air and the sunshine
and the cool green of trees and grass would do for me. The nearest place
in which I could find what I wanted was the Regent's Park. I went into one of the quiet
walks in the middle of the park, where the horses and carriages are not
allowed to go, and where old people can sun themselves, and children play, without danger.'

HESTER DETHRIDGE, FROM WILKIE COLLINS'S *MAN AND WIFE*, 1870

REGENT'S PARK

RIGHT TIME, RIGHT PLACE

RIGHT TIME, RIGHT PLACE

When George Augustus Frederick finally inherited the title of King George IV in 1820, he was 57 years old. The role had been decades in coming, a time peppered with frustration and false hopes, and the aging prince had felt the delay keenly.

Ambition had been thwarted early in life. His father, George III, had had several bouts of porphyria, a blood disorder that can affect personality changes, and as early as 1788, was incapacitated as king, leading government to consider whether young George, Prince of Wales – then only 26 – was the right candidate to rule as regent in his stead. As parliament wrangled over the question, the months rolled by, and George impatiently awaited his call. By the time a Regency Bill was finally readied for presentation to the House, George IV had recovered, and the would-be regent was just the Prince of Wales once more.

Near misses such as these can affect a person. By learning to accept the disappointment of missed opportunity early in life, the nobler of souls can take the first steps towards maturity and wisdom, realising how much they can still achieve despite their apparent loss, and by doing so, become morally greater than the role they once sought.

Alternatively, they can sulk. George soon proved himself not to be among the nobler of souls, and spent the next three decades taking the view that if he couldn't be king, then he'd at least enjoy the indulgences afforded by his role as Prince of Wales. And those not afforded, too. Within no time at all, he had run up debts amounting to two thirds of a million pounds – an extraordinary sum for the time – and had become a liability to king, parliament and country.

Meanwhile, over in Wales itself, another man was recuperating from great disappointment and a huge self-inflicted financial loss. John Nash, a Londoner and the son of a millwright, had trained as an architect and set up his own business as a young and ambitious man. While still in his 20s, he inherited a sizable sum of money, so decided to retire from architecture and move to Carmarthenshire, where he started a

It was a fine, clear, January day, wet under foot where the frost had melted, but cloudless overhead; and the Regent's Park was full of winter chirrupings and sweet with spring odours. I sat in the sun on a bench; the animal within me licking the chops of memory; the spiritual side a little drowsed, promising subsequent penitence, but not yet moved to begin.

ROBERT LOUIS STEVENSON

DR JEKYLL AND MR HYDE

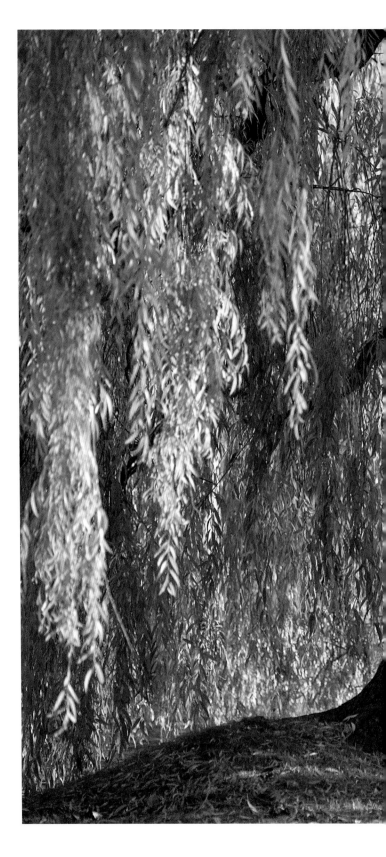

In this day before the day nobody is about.
A sea of dreams washes the edge of my green island
In the centre of the garden named after Queen Mary.
The great roses, many of them scentless,
Rule their beds like beheaded and resurrected and all silent royalty,
The only fare on my bare breakfast plate.
SYLVIA PLATH

series of dire financial investments that by 1783 had had him declared bankrupt. He was by now 31 years old, with a reputation for eccentric and rash judgement, and any chance of a glittering career seemed to be over. He took up gardening instead, and wondered about what might have been.

During this period, and for centuries beforehand, there was an area of land in London that was also biding its time, awaiting the glory days that might lie ahead. A wide expanse of wooded pasture, named after the parish church of Tybourne Village, Marylebone Park Fields had first been claimed by the crown during the reign of Henry VIII who had added it to his increasing acreage around London for his hunting pursuits. With so much fine land already at his disposal around the capital – St James's, Richmond and Bushy Parks, for example – he had no real need to add to the list, but Henry was not a man to be denied his excesses.

Yet Marylebone Park, as it became known, was some distance from Whitehall, and by the time Charles I attained the throne, it had become redundant to the Crown's uses. The doomed king mortgaged off the park to pay for the coming civil war, and once he lost that war – and his head – Cromwell appropriated the land. He, too, had debts to pay, and he promptly sold the park again, first having 3,000 trees cut down for naval construction. By the time Charles II made his return to the monarchy, many of the Royal Parks were restored to him, but he, too, could find no personal use for this excess of old Henry's, and he turned the land over to a number of tenant farmers as pasture. The family of the Duke of Portland took over the lease eventually, spending their time there enjoying the chase.

Cometh the hour

With the dawn of the nineteenth century, the area of Marylebone was becoming sought after. Residential terraced streets were appearing, and attracting members of the fashionable set who were beginning to move westwards out of the centre. Robert Harley, Earl of Oxford, had had much of the rural land turned over to housing, and hungry eyes were now beginning to turn towards the park and its potential.

Few eyes were as hungry as those of the middle-aged man who was still staring moodily out of windows and impatiently twiddling his Prince of Walesian thumbs. George's time was finally arriving, however, and it was to coincide with the era

in which Marylebone was reaching a new peak of societal status. The year was 1811, and his father had fallen to the mental ravages of his recurring blood disorder one final and lengthy time. In February, George was declared Prince Regent. Not quite king, but as good as he was to get for another nine years until George III finally died.

After such a long wait, the king-who-wasn't-quite-king needed to make his mark, and he turned to the up-and-coming Marylebone to do so, focusing his attention on the Royal-Park-that-wasn't-quite-royal. The Duke of Portland's lease ran out that same year, and the Prince Regent did not renew it. His plan was to turn London into a grander city than Napoleon's Paris, and to make Marylebone Park his own, finer than any park in London.

The first step, of course, was to rename it Regent's Park, but that was the easy bit. He then needed an architect to help him realise his vision; someone who could handle the huge responsibility laid upon him; someone who could manage the vast sums of money that would be required for this mighty venture; someone he could rely on.

He turned to John Nash.

George had not made many wise decisions in his life to date, and on face value, this one certainly wasn't going to buck the trend. Face value, however, is not always a reliable indicator. The day that the Regent who had mucked up his early life turned to the architect who had once ruined himself to revitalise the park that used to be on the wrong side of town, turned out to be one of the most significant moments in London's history.

Although George had been twiddling his thumbs since the disappointments of the 1780s, Nash had not. His gardening interest had led to a partnership with landscape architect Humphrey Repton, graduating up to working with him on the design of a number of country houses and their estates. Nash's ambition and impulsive nature had begun to return, Repton grumbling afterwards that the architect had the habit of stealing his clients. Nash had made money, however, and had returned to London to experiment further with his ideas, and

to join the social set. Trotting about London in his four-horse-drawn carriage like 'a great coxcomb', as one diarist described him, he bought a home in Dover Street and took himself a wife. Mary Anne Nash had had a previous existence, however, as a mistress of the Prince of Wales, and before long the social circles of the two men had overlapped.

Fresh with his money-laden commission to transform the old Marylebone Park and its surrounding area, Nash rolled up his sleeves. His plan was huge. He envisaged a mighty rounded park, surrounded by terraced dwellings, and containing a lake, a canal and no fewer than 56 villas settled within its grounds, along with a palace for the Regent to one side. Beyond the park, processional routes to St James's Park were planned, too, to provide George with a stretch of London bathed in monarchic glory.

Lavishly designed

Although the complete vision was never to be realised – George commissioned Nash to develop Buckingham Palace on the west side of St James's Park instead of a palatial dwelling in Regent's, only eight of the planned villas ever saw the light of day, and much of the money ran out anyway – the work

that Nash was able to complete during the second decade of the nineteenth century was still truly astonishing.

There were many, however, who felt that the Prince Regent and John Nash had been over-indulgent in their tastes. In 1842, with its tongue in cheek, *Punch* summed up the park's classical architectural mosaic: 'The houses which nearly surround the outward ring are looked upon as wonders of architectural design and execution. The liberality of the genius employed is manifested in the generous conglomeration of style which is everywhere apparent. The Corinthian and Ionic are continually contrasted with the simple Doric and the street-doric.' *Mogg's New Picture of London*, published two years later, was more cutting: 'a large portion of the property was devoted, not to the purposes of a pleasure-ground, but to a building speculation, his commission on which, with other advantages, must have been enormous.'

Today we look at it differently, the ostentatious Georgian splendour creating an opulent and charismatic tone to that stretch of London. But the austerity of the Victorian era was not so sure: the feeling was that grand though the architecture was, the park buildings and those that surrounded it had been

ACTION STATIONS:

FROM BIRD-FEEDING TO GOAL-

KEEPING, REGENT'S PARK IS A HIVE

OF ACTIVITY FOR ALL TASTES

The flowers in Regent's Park, in
spring and early summer, are a
yearly marvel and a delight.
Crocuses, scillas, and snowdrops,
too, are scattered here and there,
with a charming air of lavishness,
over the grassy slopes; this has a
delightful effect, giving all the look
and suggestion of wild flowers.

MRS E T COOK
HIGHWAYS & BYWAYS
IN LONDON, 1903

designed not for the public good, but for two selfish men to show off their wealth and prestige.

Yet for all that, there was still a park among the architecture, and if one looked away from the buildings themselves for a moment, it was indeed becoming the 'pleasure ground' desired by Mogg and many others. In 1835, the east side was opened to the public, as part of the government's drive to provide open-air facilities for the less well off, and within the next few years, heavy transformation of the park took place. The Royal Botanic Society created a lake, main lawn and special nurseries within the Inner Circle, together with a magnificent conservatory by Decimus Burton, who lived in the park; Primrose Hill was added to the park's overall acreage; Prince Albert himself developed a series of gardens at the foot of the Broad Walk; and by 1845, the general public were allowed full access to the park on two days per week. Winter skating on the Boating Lake became very popular – although disaster was to strike in 1867 when the ice broke and 40 people drowned.

By now, though, Regent's Park had a famous new highlight. In 1849, a few years after it had been opened to the public,

168,895 visitors each paid their shilling entrance fee, and spent a day wandering in fascination and awe around the various exhibits of the Zoological Gardens of London.

For many Londoners, of course, the zoo was their first opportunity of a glimpse of the exotic creatures of the world, and many of them came with preconceived ideas. *Punch* again: 'Many persons thought the Hippopotamus was a regular sea-horse, kept expressly for running in harness in a sea-captain's gig; but as the creature turns out to be very like a hog, there are many who go the entire animal in finding fault with him.'

Yet in general, the zoo was a great success, and as the years passed, people found they couldn't get enough of these curious animals and their entertaining habits, returning time and again to watch them feed and cavort. In 1881, Richard Rowe was out wandering around Regent's Park, when he heard a shout go up. As he recorded in his book *Life in the London Streets*: 'A rumour was abroad that one of the elephants or a rhinoceros was taking a bath. A little rush was made to the railings of the Zoological Gardens. Little children were perched upon the top of them; small boys shinned up them; small men held on to them. Cabmen stood on the tops of their

cabs, water-cart-men on the tops of their watercarts, drivers of waiting wagonettes on the box-seats of their vehicles, and with craning necks peered into the gardens, from which the passer-by, too lazy to cross the road, could hear ever and anon an asthmatic snorting and a ponderous splash, followed by a high-mounting sun-gilt spray. Other sight-seers "on the cheap" peered into the gardens at the turnstiles, wondering how the few neither rich nor rare personages – not a whit better dressed than themselves – whom they saw wandering about within, got there.'

Where once the park had been an opportunity for John Nash to experiment with building styles, so the zoo became the new architects' playground. Decimus Burton was responsible for the initial layout of the zoo's grounds in the late 1820s, his giraffe house with its 5m high doors one of the stand-out features. In later years, Peter Chalmers-Mitchell (Mappin Terraces, 1914), Berthold Lubetkin (Penguin Pool, 1934), Hugh Casson (Elephant House, 1965) and Lord Snowdon (Snowdon Aviary, 1964) would all make their contribution to the zoo's eclectic architectural mix.

The twentieth century also saw the first flowering of Queen

It was a beautiful September evening, windless, very peaceful. The park and the old, cream-painted houses facing it basked in the golden light of sunset. There were many sounds but no noises. The cries of playing children and the whirr of London's traffic seemed quieter than usual, as if softened by the evening's gentleness. Birds were singing their last song of the day, and further along the Circle, at the house where a great composer lived, someone was playing the piano.

DODIE SMITH
THE HUNDRED AND ONE DALMATIANS

Mary's Gardens, planted in the 1930s within the Inner Circle when the Royal Botanic Society's lease was not renewed, and the first dramatic performance of the Open Air Theatre in 1932. Sporting facilities began to be added, such as a golf and tennis school, and Regent's Park had become a true playground and entertainment venue for Londoners and tourists alike.

The war created a hiatus, the military seconding the park for encampments, and created several craters, too. More than 300 bombs fell on its grounds during the early 1940s.

The hiatus was comparatively short-lived, however, and today, the park is once again a playground for the people. It contains London's largest outdoor sports area, providing enthusiasts of cricket, football, rugby and athletics the opportunity to watch or participate during a London afternoon. Puppet theatres entertain, ducks wait to be fed and bandstands throw concerts, while several cafés and

restaurants, including the newly styled Garden Café, provide refreshment all around the park. Primrose Hill, on the other side of the Prince Albert Road, is similarly equipped with a sports pitch, and provides for those less inclined to the more active pursuits, wonderful views and delightful landscapes simply to stroll around.

Yet wherever you look, there is a reminder of the Regency age – and there always will be. There is not a lamppost, railing or bollard within the park and its terraces that is not on the government's Grade One preservation list. The park is surrounded by reminders of an age of self-indulgent wealth, yet it is also a reminder, in its remarkable range of facilities and entertainments, of what a good people's park can be.

It was a modern park in the early nineteenth century, just as it is today in the early twenty-first century. For 200 years, Regent's Park has been the park of its time.

Greenwich Park

'Greenwich Park is a jolly good place to play in,
especially the parts that aren't near Greenwich. The parts
near the Heath are first-rate. I often
wish the Park was nearer our house; but I suppose a
Park is a difficult thing to move.'

E NESBIT, *THE STORY OF THE TREASURE SEEKERS*, **1899**

GREENWICH PARK

THE HIGHER
GROUND

THE HIGHER GROUND

It has been written that 'no pessimist ever discovered the secret of the stars or sailed an uncharted land, or opened a new doorway for the human spirit.' These words are certainly inspirational, even more so when one considers that they would not have come lightly to their author. They were by Helen Keller, the American campaigner who knew a thing or two about the courage of the spirit. From a veil of blindness and deafness she emerged a leading global humanitarian, championing the rights of the disadvantaged wherever she went.

In 1946, with her companion Polly Thomson, she made her first world tour to promote the American Foundation for the Overseas Blind, stopping off in London en route. As they explored the British capital by taxi, Polly acted as her eyes and ears, relaying to her the sights and sounds of a city regrouping itself after the war. Her exact route is not recorded, but of all the sites, buildings, hubs of energy, creativity and commerce that she would have visited, none, surely, could have better matched her own summation of human positivity than London's Royal Park with a view, Greenwich Park.

The Royal Observatory and its search for 'the secret of the stars' has been a landmark of the park since 1675; the National Maritime Museum, which lies on its north boundary, has been showcasing Britons sailing to 'uncharted lands' since its opening in 1937; and of course the park itself, with its magnificent views of London and its network of tree-lined avenues, is truly an open 'doorway for the human spirit'.

Rather appropriately, the park first came into being, back in the fifteenth century, under the aegis of another humanitarian, Humphrey, Duke of Gloucester, the brother of Henry V. Although some historians now question the epithet, suggesting that his politics were not quite as sound as they were once believed to be, 'Good Duke Humphrey' was a learned soul who offered himself as a patron to study and endeavour, and founded what has now become the Bodleian Library at Oxford.

Humphrey enclosed his newly granted land in 1433, and was soon granted the right to develop a 'Manor of Greenwich to embattle and build with stone, and to enclose and make a tower and ditch within the same, and a certain tower within

GENERAL JAMES WOLFE
COMMANDS A MAGNIFICENT
VIEW FROM GREENWICH PARK

his park to build and edify'. Launched as it had been by a man of vision, Greenwich Park was never to look back, and through the centuries has cast its eyes across the myriad disciplines of science and discovery.

What a magnificent position it is able to boast for such a view. Rising above the Thames on a two-stepped hill that reaches the plateau of Blackheath, it provided a vantage point across the river for various settlements through the ages, including those of the Romans (the remains of a temple from this time still exist) and later the Saxons, who named the point Grenevic, or Green Village.

Tudor playground

Humphrey was not to enjoy his vantage point for long, dying in 1447 in prison where he was serving out time on treasonous charges. If vision had been an early feature of his park's creation, pleasure was to become its function for the next couple of centuries. The rural nature of the park made it an ideal hunting ground for a succession of monarchs, while old Humphrey's house was named the Manor of Plesaunce, or more simply, Placentia.

And very pleasant it was, too. Henry VIII was born there, and its close proximity to the royal shipyards on the Thames – which Henry in particular loved – made it a regular Tudor hangout. He married two of his wives at Placentia, or Greenwich Palace, as it was by now known, and his daughters Mary and Elizabeth were both born there. (Fascinatingly, the palace's chapel was rediscovered during drainage work in 2006 after being thought lost for 300 years). Greenwich had become the playground of kings and queens, although like all playgrounds, it had its ups and downs. One such down was experienced by Henry himself, who introduced many new aspects to his well-loved home, including stables, a banqueting hall, and amid great excitement, a tiltyard and jousting arena. Henry loved to joust; until the day came when he was unseated from his mount and hit the ground particularly hard. He lay unconscious for a couple of hours, and from that day on, in typical sulky fashion, he never jousted again. One famous, perhaps apocryphal, moment in Queen Elizabeth's life probably occurred in the environs of Greenwich Palace, too. During Tudor times, a road passed

The whole civilised world has heard of Greenwich.

JOSEPH CONRAD

THE SECRET AGENT

through the royal grounds taking travellers, who were wary of the many robbers at Blackheath, on their way from Deptford to Woolwich. This muddy road was lined by two high walls, in each of which stood a gate allowing monarchs and their guests to cross the road from the palace to the park. Some historians believe that it was here that Sir Walter Raleigh, in a gesture of gallantry and perhaps a little toadiness, famously laid down his cloak for his monarch to cross without dirtying her feet.

Greenwich had become the home of high society, and like high society, it had new fashions to follow. The European renaissance of the fifteenth and sixteenth centuries had begun to look outward in the seventeenth century, turning the continent into a hotbed of astronomic and new scientific observation. Galileo was spending his final days hoping that his heretic ideas would get past the Popish guards who had placed him under virtual house arrest; Huygens was discovering all sorts of new things about the rings of Saturn and the nature of light waves; Newton was studying prisms and refracted light and beginning to put his mind to planetary forces: suddenly the accepted views of the world and space around us were being challenged as never before.

THE SKYLINE BEHIND QUEEN'S HOUSE,
BEFORE THE BUILDING OF CANARY WHARF

On the British throne, the Stuarts were taking their turn, and when Charles II returned after the 11 years of Commonwealth, he came back enthused with the spirit of discovery that he had been surrounded by during his exile abroad.

As had many monarchs before him, he saw Greenwich as an ideal spot for his new enthusiasm. But first, he had to renovate the place. The old Tudor palace was now in a state of disrepair, the main dwelling now being the Inigo Jones-designed Queen's House on the west boundary, initially built for Queen Anne by James I, and completed by Charles I for his wife. Yet the house stood empty. During Cromwell's tenure, parliament had decided to sell off the park, but had changed its mind, reserving it instead for the Protector who never in the end lived there.

Charles got to work. In 1662, he founded the Royal Society to develop the discipline of science in the nation and get the show on the road. Turning his attention to Greenwich, he re-landscaped the park in the French style to give it the formality he felt it needed if it was to become the haven for discovery that he was looking for. And then he turned to Sir Christopher Wren. Wren was one of the founding members of the Royal Society, and the architect behind the renovation of London's

churches and cathedrals after the Great Fire of 1666. Who better, decided Charles, to create an observatory for the exploration of the stars than this singular man of vision? The commission was duly made in 1675, and the result was Britain's first purpose-built scientific research facility. It was named Flamsteed House after John of that name, the first Astronomer Royal. Although many departments of the Royal Greenwich Observatory were evacuated out of London during the World War II, and were finally closed in 1998, the building still stands today as a monument to the exploration of space and time, exhibiting an excellent array of astronomical and navigational tools, as well as famously housing the Prime Meridian, the mark of Greenwich Mean Time.

Flamsteed House and its observatory are not the only survivors of Charles's renovation of Greenwich. The landscaping by André Le Nôtre is still evident today, as are many of the trees that were planted to provide avenues for perambulatory discussion and contemplation. These avenues, planted mainly with chestnut and elm, still contain 350-year-old chestnuts that have weathered the centuries, although all of the elms succumbed to the ravages of Dutch elm disease in the 1960s and 1970s.

The rest of my cattle I got safe ashore, and set them a-grazing in a bowling-green at Greenwich, where the fineness of the grass made them feed very heartily, though I had always feared the contrary.

JONATHAN SWIFT

GULLIVER'S TRAVELS

The park has been the inspiration of many over the years. Horace Walpole MP, the historian, playwright and publisher, was 38 years old when he first discovered it, and could not believe what he had been missing. 'Would you believe,' he said to his friend Richard Bentley in 1755, 'I had never been in Greenwich Park? I never had, and am transported. Even the glories of Richmond and Twickenham hide their diminished heads.'

Naval gazing

Although the park had become a spiritual home for scientists and artists seeking enlightenment and their muse, it was not theirs alone. Royal interest in the park began to ebb after Charles's death, and when Anne came to the throne in the early eighteenth century, she opened the park up to the public. Many of the local public, of course, were involved in the naval trade, the docks being nearby, Wren's Royal Naval Hospital finally being completed (now the site of the Old Royal Naval College), and the many nearby bars ringing to the sound of maritime yarns, celebrations and ribaldry. The heady homecoming atmosphere often spilled out onto the streets of Greenwich, and now it entered the park itself, culminating twice a year in the Greenwich Fair, a raucous fiesta that rang out during May and October. The novelist Charles Dickens was rather fond of them and wrote about them in 1836 in his *Sketches by Boz*:

'The chief place of resort in the daytime, after the public-houses, is the park, in which the principal amusement is to drag young ladies up the steep hill which leads to the Observatory, and then drag them down again, at the very top of their speed, greatly to the derangement of their curls and bonnet-caps, and much to the edification of lookers-on from below. "Kiss in the Ring", and "Threading my Grandmother's Needle", too, are sports which receive their full share of patronage. Love-sick swains, under the influence of gin-and-water, and the tender passion, become violently affectionate: and the fair objects of their regard enhance the value of stolen kisses, by a vast deal of struggling, and holding down of heads, and cries of "Oh! Ha' done, then, "George – Oh, do tickle him for me, Mary – Well, I never!" and similar Lucretian ejaculations. Little old men and women, with a small basket under one arm, and a wine-glass, without a foot, in the other hand, tender "a drop o' the right sort" to the different groups;

HENRY MOORE STATUARY

The spot I had chosen for my
observations was the top of a large,
flat boulder which rose six or eight feet
above the turf. This spot I called
Greenwich. The boulder was the 'Royal
Observatory'. I had made a start! I
cannot tell you what a sense of relief
was imparted to me by the simple fact
that there was at least one spot within
Pellucidar with a familiar name and a
place upon a map. It was with almost
childish joy that I made a little circle in
my note-book and traced the word
Greenwich beside it.

EDGAR RICE BURROUGHS
PELLUCIDAR

and young ladies, who are persuaded to indulge in a drop of
the aforesaid right sort, display a pleasing degree of reluctance
to taste it, and cough afterwards with great propriety.'

Despite this coy reluctance, plenty of the 'right sort' was
indeed drunk, and in 1857 the fairs were finally closed down
as public disturbances that offended the Victorian sense
of morality.

The naval nature of the area reached a peak during the early
part of the nineteenth century once the brutal sea-battles of
Trafalgar et al got underway. So devastated were so many
families by the loss of life that Caroline of Brunswick, wife of
the Prince Regent, turned the Queen's House into a 'naval
asylum school' for the children of seamen. The school,
renamed the Royal Hospital School in 1821, only moved out in
1933, and four years later the old house was reopened as the
National Maritime Museum. Today, it is still fitted with
original and replica seventeenth-century furnishings, art,
sculpture and carvings.

After these heady times, the park continued through the late
nineteenth and early twentieth centuries in a more peaceful

manner, revamping itself steadily and quietly. Where there
was once a well-stocked deer park for the purposes of
hunting, there became a wilderness where deer can roam
freely and safely. Where once were held raucous parties with
no holds barred, there emerged a Lovers' Walk for more
genteel pursuits of amour. Where statues of military
powerhouses once took precedence, it is the works of a
sculptor like Henry Moore that now have more appeal. Even
the World War II was kinder to the park than to many others,
its main offence being to cut off the tops of some trees to
provide a wider field of view for the anti-aircraft guns that
were fitted in the Flower Garden.

But in the last few decades, Greenwich Park has taken off once
more. It has been the site of scientific discovery, and the site of
pleasure. Now, it has become a new hub of activity, as the
sporting world has claimed it for a very special niche in
history. Every year since 1981, millions of people have
watched thousands of runners launch themselves from
Greenwich Park into one of the world's most popular sporting
events, the London Marathon. And in 2012, it is due for even
further recognition when it hosts one of the key events in the
much-anticipated London Olympics.

Whether it be through science, art or sport, Greenwich Park has long had an exuberant role to play in British life, and it continues to do so. It is a place where men and women of vision and energy have laid out their plans and taken great strides forward. The first of the Royal Parks to be enclosed, it has also been perhaps the most open-minded of them all. It is truly, in Helen Keller's words, a 'doorway for the human spirit'.

But to finish, there is one tale left to be told.

Across the park from the grandeur of Queen's House stands a building in the southern corner more modest in outlook but nonetheless ambitious in nature. Various members of the royal family had held the title of Ranger of Greenwich Park through the eighteenth century, and when Montagu House, which was where some of them based themselves, was demolished in 1815, Chesterfield House was purchased in the southern corner of the park, and became the new Ranger's House. Throughout the nineteenth century, a succession of aristocrats

took over the rangership and lived in the home, until 1899, when the building was bought by London County Council and turned eventually into an English Heritage property.

Of the various rangers during that time, one in particular stands out. Between 1816 and 1844, the title was held by a woman named Sophia, who died at her post at the age of 71. She never married, nor had children, devoting herself to her role as ranger, to the park around her, and to the people who lived nearby, to whom she donated much charity. By all accounts a sprightly and energetic soul, she had a great enthusiasm for life, and upon her death, she was greatly mourned, the royal standard hoisted half-mast on Greenwich hospital, the observatory and local churches, Prince Albert attending her funeral.

But then such royal recognition was not surprising. Sophia's title was Princess Sophia, so given because she was the daughter of the Duke of Gloucester. Old 'Good Duke Humphrey' would have been proud.

Richmond Park

'Spring is good, but it's best in the autumn

when the deer are barking.

I like walking in Richmond Park and singing to

myself and knowing it doesn't matter

a damn to anybody. I like seeing things go on,

I love the freedom of it – it's like

being the wind or the sea.'

RACHEL, FROM VIRGINIA WOOLF'S *THE VOYAGE OUT*, 1915

RICHMOND PARK

WHERE LONDON STOPS

WHERE LONDON STOPS

An eleventh-century castle, a waterfall, Britain's oldest Georgian theatre, markets and tea shops nestling on the banks of a beautiful river that runs through the town: there are plenty of reasons for visiting Richmond today, as you escape the hurly-burly of London life for the more peaceful pursuits of a site of great heritage and charm.

The only thing is, you'd have to travel about 200 miles to do it. This Richmond is in Yorkshire, named by the Normans 'Riche-mont', or 'strong hill', and later an English stronghold against the perceived fourteenth-century threat of the marauding Scots. It has also been the seat of the Earl of Richmond, a title created many times over the centuries, and bestowed variously upon such luminaries as John I, Duke of Brittany (known as 'the red' due to the colour of his beard), John of Gaunt, the effective ruler of England during Richard II's minority, and the magnificently titled Conan IV who at one time allied himself with King Henry II.

But it was the tenth creation of the earldom that was the most famous, and perhaps curious, of all: famous, because it was bestowed upon Edmund Tudor, who was later to father Henry VII; curious, because Edmund was a descendant of the House of Lancaster.

Upon Edmund's death, Henry inherited the title, and went on to claim the kingdom after defeating the Yorkist Richard III at Bosworth in 1485. With the House of Lancaster back on the throne, Henry strengthened his position by marrying Elizabeth of York and unifying the two warring houses. The Tudors were now well ensconced.

But Henry hadn't quite finished. His royal home at the Manor of Sheen on the Thames in west London was a particular favourite of his. The river ran through at a gentle pace, there was fine hunting to be had across its lands, it was discretely removed from the busy centre of the capital and it stood on raised ground affording him fine views of the neighbourhood. Partly as nod to his former Yorkist enemies, mainly out of respect for his favourite earldom, he decreed that the Manor of Sheen no longer be so called, and England acquired its second Richmond. Once Henry had built a fine palace in the manor – 'an earthly

The difference in that respect of Richmond and London was enough to make the whole difference of seeing him always and seeing him never. Sixteen miles, nay, eighteen, it must be full eighteen to Manchester Street was a serious obstacle. Were he ever able to get away, the day would be spent in coming and returning. There was no comfort in having him in London; he might as well be at Enscombe; but Richmond was the very distance for easy intercourse. Better than nearer!

JANE AUSTEN

EMMA

Beginning with the Greeks, who had, he said, many difficulties to contend with, he continued with the Romans, passed to England and the right method, which speedily became the wrong method, and wound up with such a fury of denunciation directed against the road-makers of the present day in general, and the road-makers of Richmond Park in particular, where Mr. Pepper had the habit of cycling every morning before breakfast, that the spoons fairly jingled against the coffee cups, and the insides of at least four rolls mounted in a heap beside Mr. Pepper's plate.

'Pebbles!' he concluded, viciously dropping another bread pellet upon the heap. 'The roads of England are mended with pebbles!'

VIRGINIA WOOLF
THE VOYAGE OUT

paradise, most glorious to behold' – Richmond became a Tudor favourite, its hunting lands providing them with great sport, and its distance – some 10 miles – from the centre of London, turning it into an effective country retreat.

Although much of the palace was to be destroyed by Cromwell during the 1650s, the gatehouse still remains today, complete with Henry's arms upon the arch. It must have been quite a sight. Built on the same spot as its medieval predecessor that had burned down in 1497, it contained fountains, orchards, great statues, two-storey walks around the gardens, azure ceilings, rich tapestries and vast murals. Richmond Palace was the perfect place to retire to from the anxieties and inconveniences of regal life.

Henry VIII, of course, encountered many anxieties and inconveniences during his somewhat turbulent reign, not the least being his struggle to father a male heir. Frustrated with Anne Boleyn's repeated miscarriages, he made up a lame excuse to get rid of her: 'I was seduced into this marriage and forced into it by sorcery.' It is said, although probably apocryphally, that he later hightailed it to Richmond, where he stood upon its highest hill and watched for the rocket signal

that she had been beheaded. True or not, it would have been rather appropriate, as 'King Henry's Mound', as the spot is known today, is not only the highest point in Richmond Park (on a clear day you can see St Paul's Cathedral) but also a prehistoric burial mound.

(Incidentally, this high point isn't just a good place to look out for signs of renewed regal singleness, it's also pretty useful for scanning the sky for Martians. HG Wells, in his sci-fi epic *War of the Worlds*, used the peaks of Richmond as a defence against the invading aliens: 'That flicker in the sky tells of the gathering storm,' he wrote. 'Yonder, I take it are the Martians, and Londonward, where those hills rise about Richmond and Kingston and the trees give cover, earthworks are being thrown up and guns are being placed. Presently the Martians will be coming this way again.')

Back in those pre-spaceship days, Henry was often to be found at Richmond Palace, spending his first Christmas as king there and overseeing one of many jousts on the green. His daughter Elizabeth often visited its verdant expanses, too, enjoying many happy times there, and even choosing to live out her final days at the palace.

Yet Richmond was still open land, and not yet technically a park. The Stuarts – and the plague – were to change all that.

Although the Great Plague reached its zenith in 1665, it spent many years building itself up to this peak, and in 1625, Charles I decided to move temporarily, but full-time, to Richmond to escape the threat of disease. He soon found he, too, liked it there. A man fond of the hunt, he found it provided it him with the best sport he could find near London, and so, practising the type of regal excess that would later get him into very dire trouble, he decided it wanted it all to himself.

Over the wall

By 1637, he had surrounded some 2,500 acres – still the largest patch of green land in London today – with an eight-mile wall, and declared the land his and his alone. Richmond Park had now been created, but unsurprisingly there was opposition to the scheme. Although Charles had paid fair money for the land, landowners had been forced into the sale, and they considered themselves displaced. The local public were now denied access, too – many of them had used the land to collect their firewood – and the outcry lasted for several years. Finally Charles relented and, although it was too late to stem the republican tide that was building against him, he granted public access to the lands of Richmond Park, having stepladders built alongside parts of the walls to allow people through. Even the firewood rights were restored.

Charles was not the only royal to tamper with the public's rights at Richmond Park. In 1751, George II's daughter Princess Amelia became ranger of the park, and, 'a fanatical huntress', promptly denied access once more. Again, the protests were long and loud, and it took a court case at Kingston Assizes in 1758 – brought by a most public-minded local brewer called John Lewis – to reopen the park, granting for good measure a public footway through its greenery.

The victory effectively opened the floodgates. The public swarmed into the park, partly just because they could, and a new era arrived with them. Centuries of the great chase at Richmond Park effectively ended in the mid-eighteenth century (although hunting still continued in various lesser

forms) and it had become a new country retreat for the public, not just the monarchy.

It still retained the features that had been introduced since Tudor times, which included a series of new ponds created by Charles II, and a hunting lodge built for Georges I and II from 1727. Initially known as New Lodge, and later White Lodge, this building still stands near the centre of the park at the end of Queen's Ride, and has enjoyed an illustrious history. In 1805, a series of private gardens was created for the lodge, and in the same year Lord Nelson paid a visit there to the park's deputy ranger, Lord Sidmouth. It was only six weeks before the battle of Trafalgar, and the great sea admiral settled himself in the lodge and explained his plans of attack to his host, drawing them on the dining table with a wine-soaked finger.

Bored young man

The Prince of Wales, later Edward VII, also lived at White Lodge for a while. Poor old Bertie spent much of his life being told what to do, and this tenancy was no exception. His father felt that a confined period away from the hotspots of London would do the lively teenager some good: 'As companions for him we have appointed three very distinguished young men of from twenty-three to twenty-six years of age, who are to

The day in Richmond Park was charming, for we had a regular English picnic, and I had more splendid oaks and groups of deer than I could copy, also heard a nightingale, and saw larks go up.

LOUISA MAY ALCOTT

LITTLE WOMEN

ISABELLA PLANTATION

occupy in monthly rotation a kind of equerry's place about him and from whose more intimate intercourse I anticipate no small benefit to Bertie... besides these three, only [his tutors] Mr Gibbs and Mr Tarvor will go with him to Richmond.' Bertie deemed it one of the most boring periods of his life – although presumably it put him in good practice for his long wait to be king.

Two later inhabitants of the White Lodge were the newly married Duke and Duchess of York, eventually to become King George VI and Queen Elizabeth, who moved in in 1923. The couple only managed to stay there for four years, however, partly because the lodge was expensive to maintain, but mainly because of a complete lack of privacy. By now, sightseers were thronging to Richmond Park in their droves, and the chance of spotting real royalty at home was one of the star attractions. George and Elizabeth moved out, and after a few more years the White Lodge became the home of the junior section of the Royal Ballet School.

The public had by now come to love Richmond Park. They weren't just visiting it because they could, they were visiting because they wanted to. The final hunting rights had been whittled away in the first decade of the twentieth century, and Richmond Park had effectively become a huge wildlife reserve.

Natural world

And so it remains today. The latter part of the century, a more conservation-minded time, has turned the park into a genuine wildlife sanctuary, granting it SSSI (Site of Special Scientific Interest) and NNR (National Nature Reserve) status. There are times as you walk through the woodland rows of hornbeams and beeches, or listen to the songbirds as they prepare their territories and hunt for nesting materials in the spring, that it's difficult to believe you're within the boundary of one of the busiest capital cities in the world.

This sensation is particularly strong as you walk through the delightful woodland setting of the Isabella Plantation, which is home to the National Collection of Kurume azaleas introduced from Japan in the 1920s by renowned plant collector Ernest Wilson. Carpeted with bluebells in the spring, then bursting

We came to Richmond all too soon, and our destination there was a house by the Green; a staid old house, where hoops and powder and patches, embroidered coats, rolled stockings ruffles, and swords, had had their court days many a time.

CHARLES DICKENS

GREAT EXPECTATIONS

with colourful azaleas, it launches into summer richness as the rhododendrons come to life among the gentle streams that flow through it. As the ducks float lazily across the plantation's ponds, fish flicking below the surface, nature seems to have found its place.

Particularly, of course, when you see the deer. These creatures have been a staple part of the land for as long as records have been kept, and their numbers have been kept stocked up by rangers and gamekeepers throughout the ages. Today, hundreds of them still remain across the park, of both red and fallow variety, getting on with their lives without fear of hounds or arrows, wandering through the autumnal mists of the old woodlands as they have done for centuries.

Richmond Park is now truly a sanctuary for wildlife. Its acid grassland, which is grazed by the deer, is excellent for plants and insects, and thus attracts a host of natural visitors throughout the year. Over 500 species of butterfly and moth have been identified there; rural bird species such as reed bunting, skylark and meadow pipit nest within its walls; kestrels and little owls feed on the small rodents and over 1,000 beetle species that live there; many species of

endangered fungi can be found on the ancient trees that live and die in its woodlands.

And where wildlife gathers, people follow. Richmond may be a nature reserve, but it caters for the human species, too.

A network of roads and specially designated cycle paths make it a fine site for the cyclist, while rugby matches and occasionally even polo matches form just part of the sporting calendar. The park also boasts two public 18-hole golf courses. With a range of stables close by, horse-riding is also on offer, as are many other outdoor activities, from wildlife trails to angling, orienteering pursuits to cross-country running events. For visitors with a little less energy, it's also an ideal spot for a family picnic.

Public park, private worlds

It is a public park, but it is also a very private one. It has a sense of private reflection and escape from the speed and excesses of city life, which was exemplified by grand prix driver Damon Hill, who used to wander through the park with his family after a big race, taking in the surroundings and removing himself from the pressure of his day job.

Richmond had struck us both as the best centre of operations in search of the suburban retreat which Raffles wanted, and by road, in a well-appointed, well-selected hansom, was certainly the most agreeable way of getting there.

E W HORNUNG

RAFFLES, FURTHER ADVENTURES OF THE AMATEUR CRACKSMAN

For many people, London really does stop for a bit at Richmond Park. The Yorks and the Lancasters may no longer play a role in the ownership or running of the park, but the place still provides an opportunity to slow down for a bit and smell the roses.

And there's one spot in particular that is, quite literally, a perfect benchmark of this philosophy. Ian Dury was a big part of the vibrant music scene of the 1970s and 1980s, as he barked out his light-hearted but incisive lyrics to tightly written songs about wide boys, Essex life, sex, drugs and rock and roll. Punkish yet individual, he managed to combine a cheeky chappy persona with a sense of danger, and was much mourned when cancer claimed him in 2000.

Dury loved music, art and film, but he also loved Richmond Park. 'Dad used to visit the park a few times a week over a period of years and it was very special to him, he loved it,' said his daughter Jemima after he died. 'It was one of the places where he felt he could go without being spotted all the time. There were two things, amongst others, he was very passionate about – getting out into the countryside and the availability of music.'

Today, at Poet's Corner in the grounds of Pembroke Lodge in the park, near King Henry's Mound, there's a bench that you can sit on and admire the views Dury loved so much. It's a bench with a difference, though: plug in a set of headphones, and you can sit there and listen to Dury's music without disturbing anyone else, while taking in the countryside, contemplating nature, and feeling that, even for just a little while, there's a little peace in your life.

And as befits a conservation-minded nature reserve, the musical bench is powered by solar panels.

A trip to Richmond Park does indeed provide reasons to be cheerful.

Bushy Park

'I've often thought I should like to live

at Hampton Court. It looks

so peaceful and so quiet, and it is such a dear

old place to ramble round in the

early morning before many people are about.'

JEROME K JEROME, *THREE MEN IN A BOAT*, 1889

BUSHY PARK

WAR AND PEACE

WAR AND PEACE

In 1835, the naturalist E Jesse recalled in his *Gleanings in Natural History* the following tale: 'His present Majesty, when residing in Bushy Park, had a part of the foremast of the Victory, against which Lord Nelson was standing when he received his fatal wound, deposited in a small temple in the grounds of Bushy House, from which it was afterwards removed, and placed at the upper end of the dining-room, with a bust of Lord Nelson upon it. A large shot had passed completely through this part of the mast, and while it was in the temple a pair of robins had built their nest in the shot-hole, and reared a brood of young ones. It was impossible to witness this little occurrence without reflecting on the scene of blood, and strife of war, which had occurred to produce so snug and peaceable a retreat for a nest of harmless robins.'

The writer went on to suggest that this juxtaposition of war and peace might be of interest to Wordsworth and form the basis of a sonnet. The poet never did use it, but no matter, as a snippet of joint martial and natural history, it sums up perfectly the curious dual life of Bushy Park, the second largest (after its near neighbour Richmond) of all London's Royal Parks.

Today, despite being over 1,000 acres in size, it is probably the least well known of all the parks, but has recently received lottery funding to help towards its development and restoration. It is the sleeping giant of London, which is rather fitting considering that it is also the site of an ancient Bronze Age barrow, the only such known prehistoric burial site in London. Now excavated, with the contents secured in the British Museum, the 4,000-year-old mound can be found near the Teddington Gate, smaller than its once 30m length, but still visible.

By medieval times, the land had been turned over to an extensive field system for agricultural purposes, and as the sixteenth century dawned, these fields had evolved into three distinct parks: Hare Warren, Middle Park and Old Park, and were owned by the Church. Thus they may have remained, had it not been for the perpetual struggle of those Tudor times: Henry VIII's desire for a male heir.

Mr. Myles Corbett reports a Proviso to the Act for securing the Arrears of the Soldiers, out of the Lands of the late King, Queen, or Prince. And the main Question being put; It was Resolved, &c. That the Two other Parks, called the Middle Park and Bushy Park, at Hampton Court, be excepted out of the said Act.
HOUSE OF COMMONS JOURNAL
13 JULY 1649

By 1515, Cardinal Thomas Wolsey had become one of the most powerful men in England. Lord Chancellor and chief advisor to Henry, his influence was great and his standing high in the land. Yet he over-reached himself, trying to balance power in the disciplines of both Church and Crown, when he launched a surreptitious bid to the papacy. He failed in his attempt (despite later professing that he actually had no interest in the role), but had taken his eye off the ball at home. Henry had been seeking an annulment from his marriage to Katherine of Aragon in the hunt for a son, and Wolsey initially bungled the deal. The decline from favour began, and in 1529, the cardinal was stripped of his lands. He died the following year.

Henry thus found himself owning the very pleasant former Wolseyan abode of Hampton Court, and for good measure, he snaffled the three parks that surrounded it, too, devoting Bushy Park to his beloved sport of hunting, stocking it with deer.

Now owned by royalty, the three parks were to remain distinct until 1713 when another royal advisor emerged onto the scene. Charles Montagu, First Earl of Halifax, was a man of letters,

friend of Isaac Newton, former MP, Knight of the Garter, and First Lord of the Treasury. His dual role as poet and statesman, however, still gave him time for one further deed: as Keeper of Bushy Park he united the three parks around Hampton Court into one giant tract of land, and Bushy Park as we know it today was created. He took his title seriously, rebuilding Upper Lodge in the north-west corner of the park, and constructing the short canal in the nearby Canal Plantation. The magnificent Water Gardens were developed at this time, too, and are currently being restored to their former glory.

Halifax was not to enjoy the fruits of his labour long, dying in 1715, but his son, the second earl, took over the position of park ranger, adopting in the process a rather less sociable tone. Creating a central walkway through the park, he closed the park to the public, prompting a local shoemaker, who had noticed that fewer people were now passing his shop, to take court action. A plaque reveals his success: 'Timothy Bennet; of Hampton Wick, in Middlesex, shoemaker, aged 75, 1752. This true Briton (unwilling to leave the world worse than he found it), by a vigorous application of the laws of his country in the cause of liberty, obtained a free passage through Bushy Park, which had many years been withheld from the public.'

BUSHY FACT:

WILLIAM, DUKE OF CLARENCE'S
ANNUAL SALARY IN THE LATE 1820S
AS RANGER OF BUSHY PARK:
£187 9s 8d

As one wag added, regeneration (or the renewal of souls) is a shoemaker's forte. To commemorate the event, the central walkway through Bushy Park is now named Cobbler's Walk.

There was still a fee for access, however. By the end of the eighteenth century, the Duke of Clarence had moved into Bushy House (formerly the Lower Lodge) with the actress Dora Jordan and their family of 10. Later to become William IV, he used Bushy as a nice little earner, felling many of the trees, including the old oaks that had stood since Tudor times. As king, however, he undid some of the harm, and opened the park up to free public access, and even after his death his Queen Adelaide continued to live in Bushy House, and to act as ranger.

Bushy Park, in its fullest glory, was now truly a public park. Its features, which had been largely introduced during the seventeenth century, were available for all to enjoy. The Longford River, created to provide running water for Hampton Court itself, and the various ponds throughout the park were introduced by Charles I, and linked together during the protectorate, while the Chestnut Avenue (originally adorned just with lime trees) had been created during the reign of James I.

Petrified in the park

Arguably the most famous of the features, however, was the Diana Fountain, still the park's focal point at the southern end of Chestnut Avenue. Commissioned by Charles I for his Queen, Henrietta Maria, the statue was originally sited at Somerset House, and moved to the Privy Gardens at Hampton Court during Cromwell's interregnum. Sir Christopher Wren, who redesigned the Avenue, made provisions for Diana to be moved once further to the foot of the Avenue, and although his full plans for a reshaped Bushy Park were not realised, she attained her current spot in 1713.

She is not, however, Diana. Although generally referred to as the image of the goddess of the hunt, the original intention was that the figure was to represent Arethusa, one of Diana's nymphs. According to mythology Arethusa had been resting by the river Alpheus when the river god appeared and tried to seduce her. Fleeing his attentions, she called Diana for help – thus spake Arethusa – and her goddess temporarily turned her into a fountain. Alpheus continued his search for the

nymph, tracking her down finally in Sicily where he won her love. Throw a flower into the river Alpheus, it is still said, and it will appear in the fountain of Arethusa in Sicily.

Flowers, blossom in particular, are a major part of the attraction of Bushy Park. In Queen Victoria's reign began a tradition of celebrating the magnificent blossom that adorns the 274 horse chestnuts in Chestnut Avenue every year on the Sunday closest to 11 May, an attraction that grew with the century as Londoners arrived in horse and cart and toured the park's avenues. It was the place to see and be seen, and when the penny-farthing was invented, Bushy became a popular cycling route, on one date in 1877 recorded as being 'the largest meeting of bicycle riders ever assembled'.

Touring the park by horse or cycle had become the perfect way to explore its great expanse. But there had been one person for whom nature and a horseback ride had not combined well. In 1702, while touring the park's grounds, William III's horse Sorrel had stumbled on a molehill, throwing his mount, who died of complications from the fall. The Jacobites, who were longing for their man James to ascend the throne, toasted for years the 'little gentleman in the black velvet waistcoat'.

WALK LIKE AN EGYPTIAN

AN EGYPTIAN GOOSE (ABOVE) AND
A LONE FISHERMAN (RIGHT) ENJOY
THE PEACE OF BUSHY PARK

The distant memory of William apart, though, by the end of the Victorian era Bushy Park had become for many people the ideal way to explore nature, and enjoy the calm it brings. Hampton Court was now open to the public, and could be reached by railway, and the park had become a true Victorian playground. The ethos of the time was that people required areas of recreation in which they could exercise and expand their lungs, while taking in the beneficial joys of carefully shaped yet still relatively open spaces. Folk came in their thousands – on one Sunday alone in the 1890s, 3,500 tickets were taken at Hampton Court station.

Some of the rudiments of a growing sport were even developed at the park. In 1871, the members of Teddington cricket club, looking for a winter sport to play, experimented by knocking the ball around with their bats on a football field, and in the process helped to refine the sport that would eventually become known as hockey.

This peaceful rural scene on the edge of London looked set fair to continue. There was only one obstacle in its path, however, and it was a big one: the twentieth century.

Rumble of distant guns

The first omen that things were about to change blew in with the wind in 1909, when a fierce gale brought down hundreds of the park's trees. Five years on, Europe was at war, and Bushy Park, like so much of London, was not to escape its effects. Canadian troops were stationed in the park, the Upper Lodge becoming the King's Canadian Hospital. The park was still a people's park, however, and some areas of the land were literally turned over to agriculture, allowing local people to provide their own food, while events such as the Chestnut Sunday celebrations still continued. After the war, the park hosted a camp for underprivileged children.

World War II was a different affair altogether. On 15 February 1942, an American airman named Lt Col Townsend Griffiss was flying, with British military personnel, as a passenger in a Liberator aeroplane from Cairo to England. A few miles outside of Plymouth the flight encountered two fighter planes from the Polish air force who, failing to identify the Liberator as friendly, shot it down. Griffiss had become the first

American air force casualty in the conflict in Europe, and when General Eisenhower arrived in Britain to plan the 1944 D-day landings, it was at Camp Griffiss – named in the airman's honour – that he set up base.

Flying in the troops

Camp Griffiss had been pitched in Bushy Park in 1942, being as it was close to London, yet far enough away to be used as an airfield. The Eighth Air Force first used it as their headquarters, and were soon joined by the US Strategic Air Forces. Unsurprisingly, the Chestnut Sunday celebrations were halted.

When Ike arrived in January 1944, he brought with him the key personnel of Supreme Headquarters Allied Expeditionary Forces (SHAEF), who had previously been based at Grosvenor Square, and Operation Overlord began in earnest. Campaigns of such delicacy are of course necessarily kept secret, and even the local people of Teddington had no idea that Bushy Park had become anything other than just another American military base. Wire camouflage netting surrounded the hundreds of temporary huts in which the plans were hatched, while the Diana Pond, Heron Pond and

Boating Pool were also screened from enemy view. The generals came and went by entrances in the east part of the park, the new brickwork in the perimeter wall today revealing their locations.

By the time the war was over, much of Bushy Park was still littered with the huts and paraphernalia that had played such an important role in the D-day preparations. Nature, however, cannot be denied, and with a little help from park superintendent Joseph Fisher, it began to creep back to the park. Fisher turned first to one of the woodland walks, first created in 1925, which he restructured in the late 1940s as the Waterhouse Woodland Gardens.

He also prepared many other new paths and gardens through the park to encourage the public to return, and by the late 1960s most of the reminders of war had finally been cleared away. Some still remain, yet they have been placed there lest we forget: the Canadian Glade and totem pole are in honour of the troops who suffered such injuries during the World War I conflict, while a USAAF memorial plaque near Chestnut Avenue serves to remind those who pass of the extraordinary and history-shaping events that occurred in Bushy Park.

There are some ilexes, or evergreen oaks, in Bushy Park, of a very large size, and apparently as hardy as any other tree there. The avenues in that park are perhaps the finest in Europe.

E JESSE

GLEANINGS IN NATURAL HISTORY

Nature and peace began to return: the sleeping giant began to stir, and even the Chestnut Sunday celebrations were reinstated in 1976. Yet there was still one event ahead that would reshape and threaten the park, and this time it was to be a natural one. Just as a gale had ripped so many trees from their standing about a decade into the century, so a repeat disaster was to do the same about a decade from the end. The hurricane of 1987 took a mighty toll of arboreal life, destroying over 1,300 trees, the carnage taking over three months to clear.

In the years that followed, peace finally returned to Bushy Park, and today its wide expanse is enjoyed by people and nature alike. The opportunities for sports abound, with football, cricket, rugby, tennis and of course hockey all enjoyed by sporting types throughout the year, while fishing and model boating ponds are available for the more sedentary pursuits. Furthermore, the extensive Woodland Gardens and other plantations provide delightful walks, and a chance to escape busy London life in the company of nature.

With plans afoot to restore the more formal areas of the park to their pre-war glory, perhaps Bushy Park is not so much a sleeping giant after all. On a misty autumnal morning, as you ride your horse or take a walk through the bracken-laden expanses, the park's recent history can seem like a distant memory. You truly feel that you are in a country park, where nature has always been at home, and more and more of it is taking up residence: the rare double line moth, for example, was discovered there for the first time in 2005. It is almost impossible to believe that one of the most important military manoeuvres ever devised was planned here less than a lifetime ago, where deer now gaze at you through the mists and squirrels play at your feet.

Bushy Park is more, perhaps, like a sleeping beauty.

Wildlife

'The day in Richmond Park was charming, for we had
a regular English picnic, and I had more
splendid oaks and groups of deer than I could copy, also
heard a nightingale, and saw larks go up.'

LOUISA MAY ALCOTT, *LITTLE WOMEN*, 1868

LONDON'S ROYAL PARKS

WILD ABOUT LONDON

WILD ABOUT LONDON

There was a time, long ago, when a deer was not a deer. Up until the fourteenth century, when Middle English's linguistic heritage was still heavily based on the Germanic influences of Saxon, and Old Norse references still abounded, the stags and hinds of the woodlands of England were called 'heorot'. Hrothgar, in the eleventh-century tale of Beowulf, had named his great hall Heorot after the beast, decorating it with its antlers, and perhaps hoping by association to claim aspects of the animal's character as his own: its grace, its nobility, its speed. The word had majestic connotations, and eventually became abridged in English to 'hart'.

But the word 'deer' also existed in English at that time: it was the general term for any wild animal, and even Shakespeare used it in such a context, writing in *King Lear* of 'mice, and rats, and such small deer'.

By the fifteenth century, however, the usage of 'deer' was changing, and it was due to the hunt. Where once the animal had had its own name, which made it stand out from the other creatures of the field, it steadily just came to be the animal, the one that you'd most likely kill in the chase. Its importance no longer lay in its nobility, but in the role it played for those who loved to hunt.

It is to this status of the deer that the Royal Parks owe their existence. The vast majority of their combined 5,000+ acres was acquired, as often as not by Henry VIII, as deer parks for the chase, for the hunt was the recreation of royalty in Tudor times.

So much has changed in the last five centuries, as the perception of animals has evolved. Once the targets of bow and arrow, they became symbols of power, items of curiosity, and eventually creations of nature with their own rights. While Henry and his family loved to set their dogs on wildlife, James I was especially fond of receiving exotic beasts which he would house in various menageries to show his connections with foreign lands, and by the Victorian era the remarkable diversity of the international animal kingdom was drawing oohs and aahs from the thousands of visitors each year to Britain's zoos who drew social yet anthropomorphic messages from their behaviour and ways of life. The animals they housed, meanwhile, were excellent fodder for the new scientific study of natural history that burst forward during and after the time of Darwin. The late twentieth century, of course, saw yet another revolution, as conservation muscled its way to the foreground of human/animal relationships, and a new respect began to be generated for the plants and creatures with which we share this planet.

Throughout this evolution, the Royal Parks of London have been a showcase of wildlife in the context of their times. Once a collection of deer parks and hunting grounds, many of them went on to house the various mammalian and avian symbols of international trade that were collected by the kings and queens of England, and the nineteenth-century fetish for zoos and scientific research was best exemplified by the zoo in Regent's Park.

Today, we are more environmentally minded, understanding that creatures and their habitats are interlinked and that biodiversity is essential for the successful continuation of the way of life of both animals and ourselves. The Royal Parks, once again, are among the leaders in the field, becoming magnificent examples of conservation in practice, particularly when you consider their strictly urban surroundings.

They may be in the heart and around the edge of one of the world's most populated capital cities, but the parks provide a haven for people and wildlife alike. From the deer that graze the grasslands of Bushy and Richmond Parks to the wildlife areas in the central parks that support all manner of insect life, from the great variety of birds that make their homes within the parks' boundaries to the bats that roost in many of their trees, there is always something natural and new to discover.

The following pages display just some of these delights. You'll enjoy them on the page, and you'll enjoy them even more when next you walk around the Royal Parks of London.

SEEING RED

A MAGNIFICENT RED DEER STAG LOOMS FROM THE MIST IN RICHMOND PARK

SEASONAL HERALDS

THE BLUEBELLS (FAR RIGHT) OF THE ISABELLA PLANTATION IN RICHMOND PARK ARE A SURE SIGN THAT SPRING IS IN FULL FLING, WHILE THAT MOST ICONIC OF SUMMER VISITORS, THE SWALLOW (RIGHT), IS A REGULAR SIGHT AROUND THE INSECT-FILLED LAKES OF THE ROYAL PARKS

OL' BLUE EYES

OUR PHOTOGRAPHERS ZOOM IN
FOR A MORE DETAILED VIEW OF THE
ASTONISHING WILDLIFE OF THE
ROYAL PARKS, GETTING UP NICE
AND CLOSE TO A COMMON BLUE
BUTTERFLY (LEFT) AND A BLUE-
TAILED DAMSELFLY (ABOVE)

WATER WORLD

LAKES AND PONDS ABOUND IN THE
ROYAL PARKS OF LONDON,
OFFERING IDEAL HABITATS FOR
PLANTS, SUCH AS MARSH
PENNYWORT (ABOVE) AND
ANIMALS, LIKE THIS INSECT-
HUNTING PIPISTRELLE (RIGHT).
EVEN THE NATIONALLY
THREATENED GREAT CRESTED
NEWT (LEFT) HAS MADE ITS HOME
IN RICHMOND PARK

NATURAL INDICATORS OF CHANGE

LONDON'S ROYAL PARKS PLAY AN
IMPORTANT ROLE IN THE STUDY OF
URBAN BIODIVERSITY. IN 1925, THE
ORNITHOLOGIST MAX NICHOLSON
DECIDED TO COUNT THE HOUSE
SPARROWS (RIGHT AND FAR RIGHT)
IN KENSINGTON GARDENS. HE
FOUND 2,603 OF THEM. SEVENTY-
FIVE YEARS LATER, AGED 96, HE
REPEATED THE SURVEY. THIS TIME,
THERE WERE ONLY EIGHT. BASED
ON THIS AND OTHER SURVEYS, THE
WORD WENT OUT THAT THE
SPARROW WAS IN DECLINE, AND
THE WHEELS OF CONSERVATION
WENT INTO ACTION. MEANWHILE,
THE DOUBLE LINE MOTH (ABOVE),
ONE OF BRITAIN'S RAREST SPECIES,
IS FOUND AT ONLY THREE SITES IN
SOUTH-EAST ENGLAND – AND TWO
OF THEM ARE RICHMOND AND
BUSHY PARKS

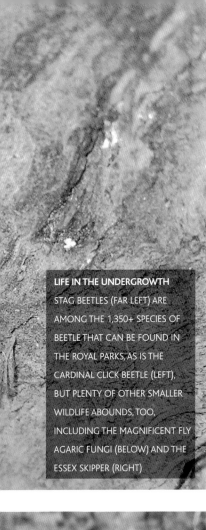

LIFE IN THE UNDERGROWTH
STAG BEETLES (FAR LEFT) ARE
AMONG THE 1,350+ SPECIES OF
BEETLE THAT CAN BE FOUND IN
THE ROYAL PARKS, AS IS THE
CARDINAL CLICK BEETLE (LEFT),
BUT PLENTY OF OTHER SMALLER
WILDLIFE ABOUNDS, TOO,
INCLUDING THE MAGNIFICENT FLY
AGARIC FUNGI (BELOW) AND THE
ESSEX SKIPPER (RIGHT)

FEEDING TIME

AN ORB-WEAVING SPIDER SPINS ITS
INTRICATE WEB IN PREPARATION
FOR FUTURE MEALS, AND A FOX
KEEPS AN EYE OPEN FOR AN
OPPORTUNITY: FEEDING TIME AT
THE PARKS IS NOT JUST CONFINED
TO THE BIG BEASTS AT REGENT'S
PARK ZOO

TAKING IT ALL IN

WHETHER IT'S THE GLIMPSE OF A
GREEN WOODPECKER (LEFT) TAKING
FLIGHT, OR THE SIGHT OF A FAMILY
OF HERONS (ABOVE) TAKING IT
EASY, THERE ARE ALWAYS PLENTY OF
NATURAL WONDERS TO SEE ON
YOUR TOUR OF THE ROYAL PARKS
OF LONDON

ROYAL PARKS INDEX

NOT ONLY, BUT ALSO...

In addition to the eight Royal Parks, The Royal Parks Foundation also helps support three other public sites in London. And like the parks themselves, these sites are rich in history and culture.

Brompton Cemetery, which was established in 1836, has a rich heritage. Among its graves can be found representatives of the breadth of experience of Victorian London: cricketing publisher John Wisden, explorer of Australia Admiral Fremantle, suffragette leader Emmeline Pankhurst and 13 holders of the Victoria Cross are all buried there, as are many of the nineteenth century London confectioner family, the Gunters.

Perhaps most intriguing among the list of names is the following roll-call: Mr Nutkin, Mr McGregor, Jeremiah Fisher, Tommy Brock – and even Peter Rabbett. It comes as no surprise, then, to discover that Beatrix Potter lived near the cemetery in her childhood years, and often took walks there.

Some living famous names have appeared here, too, the cemetery having played host to several film crews in recent years. The stars of *Goldeneye*, *Johnny English* and *The Wings of the Dove* have all been committed to celluloid at the site.

Brompton Cemetery is also rich in wildlife, and is a haven for birds, butterflies, foxes and squirrels, and over 60 species of tree.

The garden at Grosvenor Square is even older, having been owned by the Grosvenor family for centuries, although it wasn't until 1946 that it was first opened to the public. In 2003, work began on a Memorial Garden at the east end of the square, facing the American embassy, to honour those who died in the terrorist attacks on that country on 11 September, 2001.

Visitors to London may also wish to spend some time at Victoria Tower Gardens, a restful and scenic site overlooking the Thames on the southern side of the Houses of Parliament. The Gardens boast a number of statues, including a cast of Rodin's 'Burghers of Calais'. And it's not often that people visit drinking fountains other than for a drop of water, but the stunning Gothic example, the Buxton Memorial, is well worth seeing.

FILMIC SPLENDOUR AT BROMPTON CEMETERY (LEFT), THE MEMORIAL GARDEN AT GROSVENOR SQUARE (BOTTOM LEFT), AND THE BUXTON MEMORIAL FOUNTAIN AT VICTORIA TOWER GARDENS (BOTTOM RIGHT)

For further information about The Royal Parks of London simply visit www.royalparks.org.uk